IF HE ONLY HAD A BRAIN

A Collection of Opinion Pieces on the
Worst US President
EVER

Garamond 16/12/10

Cover image courtesy of Unsplash

ABOUT THIS BOOK

In our magical Land of Us, the Winged Monkeys have elected the Brainless Scarecrow as our President. Even though he has a cunning way of predicting the path of hurricanes using a sharpie—a pretty valuable power in this magical land—he simply doesn't have the right stuff to be president, because, to state the obvious . . . he doesn't have a brain.

Now it is up to the Wizards for the Rule of Law to do all they can to avoid another presidential turn for the Brainless Scarecrow, and to convince all the Cowardly Republican Lions, the Winged Monkeys and all the Munchkins in the Land of Us not to vote for him in the next 2020 elections . . .

To this end, one of these Wizards—who actually does have a brilliant brain and a flair for irony—wrote these opinion pieces, published in *USA Today* and other publications during the dark, sad "regime of the Brainless Scarecrow."

I hope that people will listen to him, and that some day, over the rainbow, this Land of Us will be again the land of sanity we all remember. At the next presidential elections, let's all close our eyes and tap our heels together three times. Let's think to ourselves, '*there's no place like what we used to call home*.' And let's vote for a candidate who *does* have a brain.

The Good Witch of the North

"With the thoughts that you'll be tweeting
You could be another Harding
If you only had a brain."

Trumped-up Justice

THE HILL - 10/11/16
By Chris Truax

At this week's presidential debate, Donald Trump invoked a child rape victim named Kathy Shelton and attacked Hillary Clinton for defending Shelton's attacker, Thomas Alfred Taylor, in court. This is a pretty important case, but not for the reasons the Trump campaign claims.

The facts are these. Back in 1976, when Clinton was a young lawyer, the trial court ordered her to defend Taylor in his criminal case. Once she was appointed as his counsel, Clinton did her best to provide her client with a vigorous defence. Eventually, Taylor pleaded guilty to a lesser offense and was sentenced to five years, with four years of that suspended. Several years ago, she did a taped interview describing the case and her involvement with it.

First, let's tackle the easy one: Trump's claim that Clinton can be heard laughing at the victim in her taped interview. It's simply false. She can be heard mildly chuckling at the some of the odd things that happened during the case, but she never laughs at the victim.

Second, Trump attacks Clinton for asking difficult questions and for asking the court to order a psychiatric examination for the victim. What Donald Trump doesn't appear to understand is that when you become the defence counsel for someone facing a criminal charge, you have an ethical duty to vigorously defend your client.

This isn't some vague notion of providing "good service" — it's expressly written into the rules. You are required to act in the best interests of your client and you aren't allowed to balance that best interest against the interests of the prosecutor, the witness, the victim — or even yourself. This sometimes means you have to ask uncomfortable questions and do uncomfortable things. Sometimes, it breaks your heart. But that's the way the system is designed to work and it's your sworn duty, so you put your personal feelings aside and do the best job you can.

But the most serious charge levelled by the Trump campaign is that Clinton agreed to take the case when she knew the client was guilty. And that is why this case is important. What I'm about to explain is one of the big reasons why the United States is the finest country in human history and not some third-rate banana republic, so pay attention.

The charge is simply unfair. The court appointed Clinton to the case, she didn't ask for it. As an officer of the court — which all lawyers are — when a court orders you to do something, you do it. Period.

But more fundamentally, defending "guilty" people is one of the most noble things a lawyer can do. In America, everybody deserves a lawyer when they are charged with a crime, guilty and the innocent alike. When a defence attorney takes an unpopular client, he or she is acting in the very finest tradition of American justice. Public defenders — who often end up taking the worst of the worst cases — are some of the finest, most ethical, most committed attorneys around. Even prosecutors will tell you so. They take these clients, not because they think they are innocent or because they want to help child rapists get back on the streets, but because they know that by forcing the system to respect the rights of even the worst of us, they are defending all of us.

Donald Trump doesn't seem to understand this, even though it is a principle so basic it is enshrined in the Bill of Rights. This worries me. It worries me a lot. Time and time again, Trump has demonstrated either ignorance or contempt when it comes to our legal system. Just tonight, he was insisting that, if he were to become president, he would make sure Clinton, his political rival, was prosecuted and sent to jail. But in America, the president does not have that kind of power. And if I have anything to say about it, he never will.

I detest Hillary Clinton. But in this case, she cannot be faulted. As a practicing lawyer myself who has, at times, defended indigent clients like Thomas Alfred Taylor, I can tell you that it is no fun working with criminal defendants, even under the best of circumstances. But no one is guilty until they are convicted. It is a great thing for a lawyer to guarantee that the legal system treats even "scumbags" fairly. That's one of the things that makes America great already.

Truax is a practicing attorney living in San Diego, and is editor of holdingournosesforhillary.com.

Legal expert: election rants, threats are pushing first amendment limits

THE HILL - 10/31/16
By Chris Truax

There's an ugly feeling in the air. A Trump supporter in Ohio, Dan Bowman, tells a reporter, "if Hillary Clinton is in office, I hope we can start a coup. She should be in prison or shot. That's how I feel about it. We're going to have a revolution and take them out of office if that's what it takes. There's going to be a lot of bloodshed. But that's what it's going to take."

An ex-house member, Joe Walsh, tweets "on November 9th, if Trump loses, I'm grabbing my musket. You in?"

Facebook, comment sections and message boards are full of angry people worrying that the vote will be "rigged" and discussing what they will do if the election is "stolen" from Donald Trump.

Free speech is an American's birthright. But for the first time in living memory, ordinary people are pushing the boundaries of the first amendment. Message boards, on-line comment sections and social media make the problem even worse. A lot of these people may think that they are just blowing off steam.

But when you are actually discussing using violence to overthrow the government or to interfere with an election, there's a very thin line between "just talk" and criminal conspiracy. In the modern world, it is perfectly possible to become a member of a criminal conspiracy by "liking" a tweet.

Conspiracy is a little different than most crimes. The essence of conspiracy is an agreement by two or more people to do something illegal. Some conspiracy statutes require that at least one of the participants take some concrete step — known as an "overt act" — toward actually carrying out the conspiracy. Some statutes do not.

Conspiring to overthrow the government by force or to "prevent, hinder, or delay the execution of any law of the United States" by force is known as "seditious conspiracy" and is punishable by 20 years in federal prison. (18 USC 2384.) Just agreeing to use force to overthrow the government or to prevent Hillary Clinton from becoming president can be a federal crime, even if you never take action.

Because seditious conspiracy is essentially speech, the first amendment comes into play. In a case called Brandenburg v. Ohio, the Supreme Court held that mere speech cannot be punished unless it is both aimed at producing "imminent lawless action" and it is likely to produce such action. So writing a book about the need for a revolution won't pass this test. Someone exhorting a crowd to burn down city hall very well might.

But "imminent" doesn't necessarily mean "immediately." Depending on the details of the conspiracy, lawless action might be "imminent" even if the conspirators understand that no violence might occur for weeks or months.

The Brandenburg test has a lot to tell us about this

election. A year ago, people on message boards and social media discussing coups and revolutions were something of a joke. No one took them seriously, probably not even themselves, so all the talk was unlikely to produce action of any sort.

But the situation is different now and might be a lot different on November 9th if millions of Donald Trump's supporters believe the election has been stolen from them. Tossing a burning match into a bucket of water isn't likely to produce a fire. Tossing a burning match into a bucket of gasoline is.

Conspiracy Law has another unpleasant wrinkle. If you enter into a conspiracy, you are guilty of every reasonably foreseeable crime that anyone in the conspiracy commits even if you, personally, have done nothing.

Let's suppose you post on a message board and you, along with dozens of other people, participate in a thread where everyone agrees, to quote Mr. Bowman, that "if Hillary Clinton's in office, I hope we can start a coup. She should be in prison or shot." Suppose someone participating in that thread tries to shoot Hillary Clinton but misses and is tackled by the Secret Service. Congratulations. You are now guilty of attempted murder.

You might think this is a fanciful scenario. It is not. The government uses theories like this regularly in terrorism prosecutions. Make no mistake. Using violence to overturn the results of an election is terrorism. And the government will treat it as such. I can guarantee that if someone does do something tragic after the election, the FBI is going to look very carefully at their social media history. Anyone found to have been egging on the perpetrator is going to find themselves in a lot of trouble they didn't expect.

The First Amendment is a national treasure. It protects our right to speak our minds without fear of government sanction. But the First Amendment also has limits. It does not protect violent conspiracy or planning bloody revolutions. It doesn't protect casual talk about the "need" to assassinate the president. Know those limits and respect them.

On November 9th, this election will be over and we will need to start putting the country back together. Start that process today. Speak out against calls for violence. Be a voice for civility and calm. Stand up for our democratic traditions. Not only will this help keep you out of trouble, it will help keep our country out of trouble.

Stay safe out there, people.

Truax is an appellate attorney in San Diego, California. He is also the editor of holdingournosesforhillary.com

Omerta: Can President Trump Really Enforce an NDA Against Steve Bannon?

The Weekly Standard, January 4, 2018
By Chris Truax

Yesterday evening, "President Donald J. Trump and Donald J. Trump for President, Inc." sent Steve Bannon a cease and desist letter threatening him with civil prosecution for "defamation by libel and slander, and breach of his written confidentiality and non-disparagement agreement." Can they really do that?

Let's do the easy one first. Donald Trump is the very definition of a public figure, so the standard in NY Times v. Sullivan applies: In order to win a defamation suit, Trump would have to prove that Bannon acted with "actual malice." In other words, he would have had to either knowingly tell lies about Trump or tell lies with reckless disregard as to whether they were true or not. As a public figure, Donald Trump would bear the burden of showing that Bannon acted with actual malice and that is a very tough standard to meet, intentionally so.

It's probably impossible in this case as, from what I have seen, most of what Bannon said seems to be either reasonably factually accurate or Bannon's opinion. Mere opinion, however, is never defamatory. Bannon's opinion that Donald Trump Jr.'s Russian meeting was treasonous might be wrong, but it's just that, an opinion and so not actionable. His opinion that Donald Trump Jr. was unpatriotic and should have reported the meeting to the FBI is also opinion—and absolutely correct to boot—and so also not actionable.

So there is no case for defamation. What about the non-disclosure and non-disparagement agreement Bannon signed? Now it gets a little weird.

Donald Trump has been famous for years for forcing his employees to sign elaborate and comically one-sided non-disclosure and non-disparagement agreements. This paranoia extended to the campaign. Any Trump volunteer who wanted to so much as phone bank from home was required to agree to a five-page contract that purported to prevent the volunteer from disclosing any confidential information for a term of, well, a term of forever. Confidential information was defined as, among other things, "all information that Mr. Trump insists remain private or confidential."

The agreement also prevented campaign volunteers from ever supporting another candidate (either in 2016 or 2020) so long as Mr. Trump remained in the race. The agreement even required campaign volunteers to prevent their employees from supporting anyone but Trump.

Finally, the agreement included a non-disparagement clause. "During the term of your service and at all times thereafter you hereby promise and agree not to demean or disparage publicly the Company, Mr. Trump, any Trump Company, any Family Member, or any Family Member Company . . . and to prevent your employees from doing so."

All of this was enforceable both through damages and injunction. Plus, the agreement gave Trump—but not the volunteer—the right to choose arbitration or to sue in court to enforce the agreement.

We can safely assume that the agreement Bannon signed has similar terms; the letter sent by his attorney suggests as much. In the private sector, much of this might well be enforceable. But Donald Trump isn't in the private sector anymore.

President Trump qua President Trump is bound by the First Amendment.

That doesn't necessarily mean that confidentiality agreements are unenforceable. The CIA enforces them all the time. The leading case describing the First Amendment contours of the government's ability to enforce confidentiality agreements is Snepp v. United States. In Snepp, an ex-CIA agent published a book—which contained no classified information—without going through the CIA's pre-approval process. While the government could not enjoin publication of the book, the Court allowed the government to seize the author's royalties.

Applying that rule to President Trump, the confidentiality agreement Bannon signed might allow for seizure of any profits Bannon made in his speech—apparently there were none—but it would not authorize any sort of injunction, or even damages.

But it probably would not allow for even that. The Snepp case turned on the government's legitimate need to review books by ex-CIA employees before publication in order to prevent the release of classified information that might endanger legitimate, on-going governmental activities. The First Amendment is that much stronger—and the government's interest that much weaker—when the information at issue is merely politically embarrassing.

Which brings us to the other potential plaintiff: Donald

J. Trump for President, Inc.

There is no question that Trump for President is a private actor and is not bound by the First Amendment. This is why Trump for President can hold rallies and throw out people who are wearing the wrong t-shirts. So as between Trump for President, and Steve Bannon, the non-disparagement agreement ought to be enforceable . . . except for the public policy exception.

Courts will not enforce contracts that violate public policy. The most obvious case is a contract for something illegal. Courts will not, for example, enforce a contract for the sale of illegal drugs. Contracts limiting speech require courts to balance competing policies. A confidentiality agreement may prevent you from generally revealing information but it cannot prevent you from speaking with law enforcement or acting as a whistleblower.

So this agreement is far from watertight. If Trump for President had sought an injunction to prevent one of its volunteers from switching their support to Ted Cruz, they would have been laughed out of court. The same goes for the non-disparagement clause. Bannon's case is slightly more complicated since he was one of the people running the campaign, rather than a volunteer. So a court might well have been inclined to enforce at least the confidentiality provisions . . . if it were October 2016.

The calculus is different in January 2018. There is a very strong public policy interest in supporting transparency in our political system and a very weak public policy interest in helping whoever happens to be in the White House avoid embarrassment.

Plus—and this is really the root of it—the whole thing stinks. There is something deeply disturbing about watching the president of the United States attempting to use the legal system to silence his critics. This is the kind of thing that "soft" despots do, not American presidents. It seems likely that any court would find that a contractual prohibition on "demeaning or disparaging" the president "at all times thereafter" is a gross violation of publicly policy and, therefore, unenforceable.

So, no, they probably can't really do that.

Chris Truax is an appellate lawyer in California.

The FBI passed its stress test

InsideSources.com, June 20, 2018
By Chris Truax

There is no doubt that the inspector general's report on the FBI's handling of the Hillary Clinton email investigation is going to be treated like a giant Rorschach test. President Trump's partisans will froth about the "deep state," while Clinton will wail about how James Comey stole the election from her.

But the inspector general's report actually makes the FBI look pretty good. The report found no evidence that anti-Trump political bias had any effect on any of the FBI's decisions. In fact, what mistakes were made can fairly be viewed as an effort to not be "pro-Clinton," even though the FBI thought Clinton was extremely likely to be elected president.

While I have questioned Comey's judgment, I have never questioned his integrity — and the inspector general's report agrees. The investigation concluded that the Clinton email probe was handled appropriately, and that its decision not to charge Clinton was reasonable and in keeping with prior practice at the Department of Justice.

Where Comey really went wrong — and he did so for the best of motives — was in his decision to discuss publicly the decision not to file charges. He felt that this unprecedented transparency — the FBI never typically discusses the details of why they have closed an investigation without filing charges — was necessary because of the "need to preserve the credibility and integrity of the department and the FBI, and the need to protect a sense of justice more broadly in the country; that things are fair, not fixed; and they're done independently.'"

The inspector general disagreed and faulted Comey's judgment but not his professionalism. "While we found no evidence that Comey's statement was the result of bias or an effort to influence the election, we did not find his justifications for issuing the statement to be reasonable or persuasive. We concluded that Comey's unilateral announcement was inconsistent with department policy and violated longstanding department practice and protocol by, among other things, criticizing Clinton's uncharged conduct."

Another sore point for President Trump and his supporters was the anti-Trump bias exhibited by some FBI agents, particularly Peter Strzok and Lisa Page, who texted their dislike of then-candidate Trump while using official FBI phones. But the key point here is not that FBI agents are humans who occasionally slip and engage in less-than-ideal behavior. The key point is that the culture of internal transparency at the FBI was an effective check on these inevitable human failings: Strozk and Paige's personal bias did not affect the decisions made by the FBI because these decisions were made as a group rather than by a single individual.

As the inspector general put it, "We found that Strzok was not the sole decision maker for any of the specific (Clinton email) investigative decisions we examined. ... We further found evidence that in some instances Strzok and Page advocated for more aggressive investigative measures in the (Clinton email) investigation, such as the use of grand jury subpoenas and search warrants to obtain evidence."

Apparently, despite their personal political views, even Strzok and Page maintained their professionalism.

The inspector general was perfectly correct to investigate how the FBI handled the momentous investigation into then-Secretary Clinton's email server. Given the stakes and the stress, it is not surprising that the inspector general concluded that some things about the investigation — especially the decision to make a public statement about the reasoning behind the decision not to charge Clinton — could have been handled better.

But the takeaway here is that the FBI, in the middle of the most contentious presidential election in living memory, managed to navigate a difficult, complex and politically charged investigation and managed to get it almost entirely right, and all without compromising its independence or, as an organization, its professionalism. Yes, the FBI made mistakes, especially Comey's decision to depart from established departmental protocol to discuss publicly the investigation. But those were errors of judgment made in good faith rather than some corrupt scheme to influence the election. And, if anything, these errors of judgment only benefitted Trump the candidate, so he has little to complain about.

The inspector general's report confirms what Americans have always believed: The FBI is made up of straight shooters who let the chips fall where they may without fear or favor. Yes, they may occasionally miss their aim, as do we all. But as a group, an institution, and a culture, they are fiercely dedicated to professionalism and upholding the rule of law even under the most difficult conditions.

Donald Trump might not like it. Hillary Clinton might not like it. But the FBI's job isn't to be liked; it's to uphold the rule of law. And, according to the inspector general, that's exactly what the FBI did.

Chris Truax is an appellate lawyer in California and sits on the legal advisory board for Republicans for the Rule of Law. He wrote this for InsideSources.com.

Don't make a deal: America needs a Mueller-Trump confrontation over rule of law

USA Today, August 13, 2018
By Chris Truax

Mueller should subpoena Trump rather than offer him special deals. Let's establish right now that all presidents are subject to courts and laws.

Mueller should subpoena Trump rather than offer him special deals. Let's establish right now that all presidents are subject to courts and laws.

Special counsel Robert Mueller has been trying hard to secure voluntary testimony from President Donald Trump as part of his investigation into Russia's interference in the 2016 presidential election. Trump's legal team, however, has rejected Mueller's latest special offer — even as Trump steps up his attacks on Mueller and his work, and effectively orders Attorney General Jeff Sessions via Twitter to fire Mueller and end the investigation.

Should Mueller make Trump an even better offer? The thinking is that even a quarter of a loaf is better than none, and that issuing an actual subpoena would certainly trigger a massive confrontation with President Trump.

Don't do it, Mr. Mueller.

By all accounts, Mueller is the opposite of reckless. It is understandable why he would want to do everything in his power to amicably resolve his "dispute" with Trump over his testimony and avoid the constitutional crisis that calling the president's bluff and issuing a subpoena would surely bring.

Confrontation would strengthen our laws
But there is more at stake in this confrontation than determining exactly how the Russians conspired to interfere with a U.S. election. As serious as that is, a threat to the rule of law is even more serious, and that is exactly what we face in Trump's persistent claims that the president is not subject to the courts.

They say what doesn't kill you makes you stronger, and that's certainly true with respect to America's legal institutions. Those institutions have been shaped through principled confrontation rather than expedient compromise going all the way back to Marbury v. Madison, which firmly established the principle of independent judicial review and is one of the cornerstones of our constitutional system of government.

That system was strengthened once again in the Watergate case. In an effort to quash the special prosecutor's subpoena seeking to force President Richard Nixon to turn over tapes, Nixon's legal team argued that the president "is as powerful a monarch as Louis XIV, only four years at a time, and is not subject to the processes of any court in the land except the court of impeachment."

But in United States v. Nixon, the Supreme Court held that the president is not a king and that he, like any other citizen, is subject to the jurisdiction of the courts. United States v. Nixon stood our country in good stead when President Bill Clinton attempted to evade his own subpoena. This time, there was no constitutional crisis. The judicial precedents established in the Nixon cases turned what could have been high drama into low farce.

And now, in his turn, President Trump is claiming that he is above the courts and outside the rule of law. Worse, there is the sense that our institutions are too fragile to withstand the shock of a confrontation between the presidency and the judiciary. If that is so, our constitutional system of government is already lost. Our institutions are not yet so weak. But they are not getting any stronger, and they will not become stronger through a failure to exercise them. If we must have this confrontation, the sooner the better. Giving Trump special treatment out of fear he will provoke a constitutional crisis by ignoring a grand jury subpoena only weakens those institutions for the next confrontation. And such a confrontation is certain to come, if not from this president then from a future one. You cannot deter bad behavior by rewarding it.

Let's have our constitutional crisis now
The president is merely a citizen entrusted with high office. While the courts must pay due deference to the president's constitutional responsibilities, he is no more entitled to violate the laws or ignore a court order than is any other citizen. Like any other citizen, he has a duty to provide evidence in response to a grand jury subpoena.
Giving evidence before the grand jury is occasionally stressful, sometimes embarrassing, but essentially simple: Tell the truth. If this is something President Trump is unable or unwilling to do, the sooner we find

out, the better.

If we are going to have a constitutional crisis to establish, once and for all, that the president of the United States is subject to the courts and the laws, let's have it now, with this president. I am not so much interested in punishing past transgressions as I am in preventing new ones. If one thing comes out of Trump's confrontation with Mueller, I hope it will be a firmly established principle that no one, including the president — especially the president — is above the law.

Chris Truax, an appellate lawyer in San Diego, is on the legal advisory board of Republicans for the Rule of Law.

Candidate Trump might have won a lawsuit to silence Omarosa. President Trump, no way.

USA Today, August 15, 2018
By Chris Truax

Trump made campaign staffers sign a comically harsh NDA. But no court would let him enforce it as president. It's un-American and anti-First Amendment.

Donald J. Trump for President, Inc. has filed a private arbitration action seeking to enforce a non-disclosure and non-disparagement agreement that had been signed by Omarosa Manigault Newman when she worked for the Trump campaign. Since then, of course, she's been hired at The White House, fired by the White House and written a book — a very critical, very embarrassing, very detailed book. Should she be worried?

The arbitration seeks to silence Omarosa, as almost everyone knows her, by enforcing a contract that Trump's presidential campaign required all staffers and volunteers to sign. Even if you wanted to volunteer to phone bank from home, you had to sign this five-page agreement.

The agreement used by the campaign was itself patterned on something President Donald Trump made all of his Trump organization employees sign. Hold on, because this gets a little weird.

The agreement used by the Trump campaign is comically harsh and one-sided. Among other things, it attempts to prevent volunteers and staffers from disclosing any confidential information for a term of forever. The agreement defines "Confidential Information" as, among other things, "all information ... that Mr. Trump insists remain private or confidential."

A president can't block free speech
Even worse, the agreement claims to prevent campaign volunteers from ever supporting another candidate so long as Trump remained in the race. It also requires campaign volunteers to prevent their employees from supporting anyone but Trump.

Finally, the agreement included a non-disparagement clause. "During the term of your service and at all times thereafter you hereby promise and agree not to demean or disparage publicly the Company, Mr. Trump, any Trump Company, any Family Member, or any Family Member Company ... and to prevent your employees from doing so."

Supposedly, this is all enforceable through both damages and an injunction. To top all this off, Trump or his campaign — but not the volunteer — has the right to choose arbitration or to sue in court to enforce the agreement.

It is possible that some of this might be enforceable in the private sector. But Trump is no longer candidate Trump. Now he's President Trump, and he's not in the private sector anymore. The First Amendment prevents a government official from enforcing non-disclosure agreements — and certainly non-disparagement agreements — against government employees. Even ex-CIA agents can write about their experiences so long as they do not reveal classified information.

Donald J. Trump for President, Inc., however, is a private actor and not restricted by the First

Amendment. This is why Trump for President can hold rallies and remove people who are wearing anti-Trump t-shirts. So in theory, Trump for President could enforce its non-disclosure and non-disparagement agreements. But it's not quite that simple.

Courts will not enforce contracts that violate public policy. For example, a court will not enforce a contract for something illegal, like selling drugs — and such an agreement can't be enforced through private arbitration, either.

Because free speech is so important, contracts limiting speech require courts to balance competing public policy interests. For example, a confidentiality agreement may prevent you from generally revealing information about a company you worked for, but it cannot prevent you from speaking with law enforcement or acting as a whistleblower.

So you can imagine that a court is going to take a long, hard look at a confidentiality and non-disparagement agreement that seeks to limit the freedom of campaign volunteers and staffers. If Trump for President had sought an injunction to prevent a volunteer from switching his or her support to Sen. Ted Cruz, it would have been laughed out of court. The same goes for the non-disparagement clause.

Maybe, just maybe, the Trump campaign could have enforced a confidentiality provision against a Trump staffer like Omarosa before the election. Campaign staff are entrusted with sensitive technical information about political strategy and a court might well have decided a campaign could prohibit a rogue employee from using that information unfairly.

Silencing critics is rotten and un-American

But the calculus is completely different now that the election is long over. This is all the more true since the Trump team is, for the most part, attempting to silence Omarosa regarding her government service. There is a very strong public interest in supporting transparency in our political system. There is no public interest at all in helping a president, whoever it may be, avoid embarrassment.

So it is pretty unlikely that a court is going to decide that the Trump campaign can enforce either the confidentiality clause or the non-disparagement clause and prevent Omarosa from ever saying anything bad about President Trump or his family. On the contrary, there is a very strong public interest in having the people helping run our government speak out about their experiences.

Bottom line: No court would allow President Trump to use a non-disparagement or confidentiality agreement to silence his critics because the entire idea is utterly rotten and un-American. A contractual prohibition on "demeaning or disparaging" the president is a gross violation of the public interest and, therefore, it would be found unenforceable.

Enjoy your book tour, Omarosa. I may not agree with what you say, but I cannot tell you how happy I am that we live in a country where not even the president can stop you from saying it.

Chris Truax, an appellate lawyer in San Diego, is on the legal advisory board of Republicans for the Rule of Law.

After Manafort conviction & Cohen plea, Donald Trump is so desperate he could do anything

USA Today, August 22, 2018
By Chris Truax

Michael Cohen knows about all the skeletons in Trump's closet. Manafort could begin to cooperate with Mueller. For Trump, this is crunch time.

One of the few things that all Americans can agree on regardless of their political leanings is that the non-stop barrage of scandal and controversy is getting exhausting. Once upon a time, August was the silly season when everyone, including politicians and reporters, took a well-deserved break and the news was dominated by stories about weekend traffic and water-skiing squirrels.

Alas, no longer. On Tuesday, in the course of less than an hour, two bombshells dropped. In more innocent days, either one would have rocked the country for months. First, after a 12-day trial, a jury found President Donald Trump's ex-campaign manager, Paul Manafort, guilty on eight felony counts involving bank fraud and tax evasion. The judge declared a mistrial on 10 other counts that could, if the prosecution chooses, be retried later. Second, Trump's former personal attorney, Michael Cohen, pleaded guilty to eight felony counts involving one count of bank fraud, five counts of tax evasion and, crucially, two felony campaign-finance violations. These last two are critical because they directly implicate the president in a felony conspiracy.

Even by current standards, this is not normal.

Trump could pardon Manafort

As shocking as it is, the Manafort case does not — at least not yet — implicate Trump in any illegal activity. But Manafort faces another trial next month and Robert Mueller, the special prosecutor tasked with investigating matters related to Russia's interference in the 2016 election, would very much like Manafort's assistance. So far, Manafort has refused to cooperate. But not, we can be sure, out of loyalty to Trump.

Now that Manafort is facing the possibility of spending the rest of his life in prison, there are two possibilities. He either fully cooperates in the hope of limiting his eventual sentence, or Trump pardons him. I have no idea what, if any, information Manafort might have that would interest Mueller. But Trump knows, and if there is any such information, Trump may well decide to pardon him and accept the political consequences.

Cohen, who was being prosecuted by the U.S. attorney's office rather than Mueller's office is, if possible, an even worse nightmare for the president.

First, while Cohen appears to have entered his guilty plea without any formal cooperation agreement with the prosecution, it seems clear he is pretty cooperative already. The two campaign-finance felonies he admitted involved paying off Stormy Daniels and Karen McDougal which, according to Cohen's guilty plea in open court, he did "in coordination with and at the direction of a candidate for federal office."

In other words, he made illegal payoffs to these women on Trump's orders.

This is bad enough. These charges aren't going to disappear. While it is extremely unlikely Trump will be indicted while he is in office — Department of Justice guidelines forbid indicting a sitting president — it is hard to imagine that the next ambitious U.S. attorney for the Southern District of New York would not prosecute these charges. Rudy Giuliani made his name as a U.S. attorney prosecuting mobsters and insider traders. Imagine prosecuting a president of the United States.

It gets worse. If anyone knows where the bodies are buried, it's Cohen. He was, after all, Trump's grave digger in chief for many years. Whatever else might be out there, it's all going to be in the hands of the U.S. attorney. Unlike Manafort, Cohen was prosecuted by the regular U.S. attorney's office, which has a mandate to investigate any federal crimes they discover, whether it has anything to do with Russia or not.

Trump could undermine the rule of law

What does all this mean? It means that if Trump has anything to panic about, he's panicking now. He's likely to do something desperate and damaging: fire Mueller; pardon Manafort; pardon himself. The only thing that has restrained him is his fear of political retribution. But now that the fear of political retribution is being replaced by the certainty of legal retribution, there is no telling what he will do.

The next several weeks are critical. If Trump is going to take steps to interfere with Mueller's investigation or subvert the justice system through use of the pardon power, it will likely be soon.

I don't know what, if anything, Trump is guilty of. But I do know that no one, including Trump, is worth sacrificing the rule of law. In a way, this is all kind of thrilling. The rule of law is the cornerstone of our constitutional system of government, one of those things we learned about in seventh grade civics class and that people like Washington, Jefferson and Madison fought for. Regardless of whether, in our opinion, Trump is being treated "fairly" or not, it is something that each one of us needs to stand up for and defend.

Because the rule of law is not a Republican or a Democrat thing. It's not a liberal or a conservative thing. It's an American thing.

Chris Truax, an appellate lawyer in San Diego, is on the legal advisory board of Republicans for the Rule of Law.

Trump Twitter attack on Sessions and Justice is most serious impeachment fodder yet

USA Today, September 4, 2018

By Chris Truax

Donald Trump's attack on Jeff Sessions for not politicizing the Justice Department is the single most serious, potentially impeachable thing he has ever done.

That's it. Line crossed.

It came Monday when President Donald Trump tweeted: "Two long running, Obama era, investigations of two very popular Republican Congressmen were brought to a well publicized charge, just ahead of the Mid-Terms, by the Jeff Sessions Justice Department. Two easy wins now in doubt because there is not enough time. Good job Jeff......"

In other words, President Trump is now angry that Attorney General Sessions did not put party politics ahead of enforcing the law. He thinks that the Justice Department should have suppressed the charges against Reps. Chris Collins of New York and Duncan Hunter of California because bringing those charges might cost Republicans two safe House seats.

This is exactly what the rule of law does not look like.

When it comes to enforcing the law, it should be — and, up until now, it has been — completely irrelevant whether a politician was "popular" or "Republican," how close it was to the midterms or even whether the target of the investigation was going to have an "easy win." The Justice Department carries out its investigations with all deliberate speed and files criminal charges as appropriate, all without giving any consideration as to who might be helped and who might be hindered by the impartial enforcement of the laws.

Party politics instead of justice and law
This is not the department's first rodeo. It has a long history of prosecuting members of Congress and detailed procedures to ensure it does so impartially. A member of Congress cannot even be investigated, much less charged, until the U.S. attorney's office consults with the Justice Department's Public Integrity Section.

On top of that, both U.S. attorneys bringing the cases are Trump administration appointees. This is not a partisan "witch hunt," even though Trump tries to make it sound like one by claiming these charges were the result of "two long running Obama era investigations." While the investigation into Hunter has been ongoing — and widely reported —since April of 2016, the charges against Collins have nothing at all to do with Obama because they all relate to crimes that allegedly occurred in June 2017.

Politically, Hunter's situation is a carbon copy of what happened to Rep. Dan Rostenkowski, the powerful head of the Ways and Means Committee indicted by the Justice Department. This was back in the 1990s, and it was Democrat Bill Clinton's administration that prosecuted Rostenkowski, an Illinois Democrat.

Amid a well-publicized corruption investigation, Rostenkowski won his primary. As in Hunter's case, Justice filed formal criminal charges after the primary but before the general election. Despite what was supposedly a safe seat — Rostenkowski's Chicago constituents had not elected a Republican for 35 years — he lost the general election and eventually went to prison.

So the idea that Justice is doing something outrageous by prosecuting a couple of "popular" congressmen from the president's own party "just ahead of the midterms" is ridiculous. It's not outrageous. It's standard operating procedure, and it has been for many decades.

What is outrageous is Trump's assumption that Justice should be politicized. It seems odd to have to make the case for the rule of law, but these are odd times. Whether you support Trump or not, you should be horrified by the idea that the Justice Department ought to protect the president's friends and punish his enemies. Now that it is Trump running the show, you might think it's a fine idea. When, say, Elizabeth Warren is president and decides to follow Trump's example and weaponize the Justice Department, how will you feel then?

Tweet is most impeachable Trump action to date

If you do support Trump and his agenda, there is another reason to speak up for a Justice Department that enforces the law without fear or favor. It is because Trump's tweet castigating Sessions for not politicizing the department is the single most serious and potentially impeachable thing he has ever done. He is denigrating — worse, he simply has no conception of — one of the cornerstones of our entire constitutional system of government.

If Trump wants to have any hope of completing his term, much less getting re-elected, he must be quickly and sharply educated. If he is not, he will eventually act on what to him seems a perfectly natural and logical idea: that the Justice Department exists to do his personal bidding. Should that happen, it would be a disaster, both for America's political system and Trump's presidency. He needs to be forced back from the brink, before it is too late.

Placing some clear limits on Trump is in everyone's interest, and Congress needs to take immediate steps to make its displeasure known. Perhaps it could pass a joint resolution condemning Trump's tweet and affirming the necessity of an apolitical Justice Department.

In addition to defending the rule of law, such a resolution would help separate the sheep from the goats. Anyone in Congress who is not "brave" enough to take a public stand against turning the Justice Department into the enforcement arm of a new Committee to Re-elect the President has no business in public life.

Much has changed over the past few years, and many things we have taken for granted are now in question. But one thing we cannot allow to be normalized, one line we cannot cross, is the corruption of our justice system. No matter what.

Chris Truax, an appellate lawyer in San Diego, is on the legal advisory board of Republicans for the Rule of Law.

Jeff Sessions Is Acting Like Donald Trump's Thomas Becket

The Weekly Standard, September 12, 2018

By Chris Truax

Lessons of fidelity to something greater than a ruler.

In 1162, King Henry II of England made Thomas Becket the Archbishop of Canterbury and the leader of the English Catholic Church. Becket, one of Henry's most loyal supporters, had been the king's Chancellor. Henry assumed that, with Becket in charge, the Church would cease to be a thorn in his side and instead become a pillar of support for his rule.

Becket was ambitious, a bit of a medieval party animal, and, prior to his elevation, showed little sign of having any principles at all, much less religious ones. He was only ordained as a priest on the day before he became Archbishop.

But much to everyone's surprise—probably including Becket himself—Thomas Becket got religion. Rather than becoming Henry's tool and helping him bend the Church to his whims, Becket became an outspoken and aggressive advocate for the Church's rights and interests.

The king was first bemused, then furious. Somehow, Becket had found his moral compass. When Becket was the King's man and his Chancellor, he sought to please him in all things. But when Henry made him head of the Catholic Church, he was forced to accept higher loyalties.

"You know how long and loyally I served the king in his

35

worldly affairs. For that cause, it pleased him to promote me to the office which now I hold. When I consented, it was for the sake of the king alone," said Becket. "When I was elected, I was formally acquitted of my responsibilities for all that I had done as a chancellor."

Thomas Becket became Archbishop of Canterbury by order of the King. But once he had become Archbishop, he was no longer the King's to command.

In many ways, American lawyers have much in common with medieval priests. Like them, American lawyers are initiated into a long tradition filled with arcane and powerful knowledge. The law, like religion, has its own profound moral code that may be baffling to outsiders.

It's a popular suspicion that lawyers have no ethics. In reality, they are trained in a rigorous ethical system that values things which, to the layman, may seem odd, like independent judgment and fair procedures rather than "morally correct" results. It is also an ethical code that is based, unusually, on humility. An American legal education is devoted to the proposition that there are at least two sides to every question and that there are no right answers, only valid arguments.

Consequently, since they know that the "correct" result is always debatable, lawyers place their faith in fair procedures above all. And they can be passionately attached to their principles even when they are not in their best interests.

It is no surprise that the main line of defence against President Donald Trump's efforts to warp our justice system has been Republican lawyers appointed by Trump himself. These lawyers value the rule of law, an independent judiciary, and a fair and apolitical justice system far more than they value their careers.

Lawyers, of course, are human and often fail their creed. But even as they violate them, they know that they are falling short of the standards they have been trained to respect.

Jeff Sessions was one of Donald Trump's most ardent supporters and perfectly happy to abandon a lifetime of conservative principles for a ride on the Trump train. Like Becket, Sessions was willing to do almost anything to please his political master. He defended Trump's indiscretions, made excuses for his failings, and publicly praised him in the most nauseating terms. He even wore a MAGA hat.

But when Senator Sessions became Attorney General Sessions, like Archbishop Becket, he got religion. It is one thing to clown around on the sidelines, but when you become the latest in a long line of lawyers entrusted with enforcing the laws and defending the Constitution, it changes you.

Senator Sessions seemed willing to say or do anything that seemed politically expedient. But Attorney General Sessions has, most often, done the right thing, even at great political cost. First came his decision to recuse himself from the Russia investigation, an easy call for a lawyer to make—you may not act when you have even the appearance of a conflict of interest—but one that President Trump still considers an unfathomable act of personal disloyalty.

The more that Trump pressured him to be "his" attorney general and politicize the Department of Justice, tear down the FBI, and end the Mueller investigation, the more Jeff Sessions seemed to live the principles he had learned so long ago in law school.

"The more I loved the king, the more I opposed his injustice until his brow fell lowering upon me. He heaped calumny after calumny on my head, and I chose to be driven out rather than to subscribe." While the sentiments are Thomas Becket's, they could just as easily have been those of Jeff Sessions.

A few weeks ago, in response to yet another presidential attack on his decision to recuse himself from the Russia investigation, Sessions responded, "While I am attorney general, the actions of the Department of Justice will not be improperly influenced by political considerations. I demand the highest standards, and where they are not met, I take action. However, no nation has a more talented, more dedicated group of law enforcement investigators and prosecutors than the United States."

Credit where credit is due: Jeff Sessions's journey from Trumpian sycophant to chief defender of the rule of law is complete. In the end, when it mattered, Jeff Sessions turned out to be a lawyer after all.

This all ended badly for Becket but quite well for the church he led. On what they believed to be King Henry's orders, four of his knights assassinated Becket. While Henry denied responsibility, he was widely blamed for Becket's death and was forced to abase himself before the power of the Church. Thomas Becket is now revered in both the Catholic and the Anglican churches and is considered to be one of the outstanding figures in English history. While Jeff Sessions will eventually be dispatched by the tweet rather than the sword, may his ending be as worthy.

Chris Truax, an appellate lawyer in San Diego, is on the legal advisory board of Republicans for the Rule of Law.

Protect Mueller and Rosenstein. It's a 'Profiles in Courage' moment in American history.

USA Today, September 26, 2018
By Chris Truax

Protect Mueller's Russia investigation. It's not just about Trump or even mostly about Trump. It's about a very well-documented attack on our democracy.

President Donald Trump is thinking of firing Deputy Attorney General Rod Rosenstein based on leaked memos about two tense meetings he had in 2017 with Andrew McCabe, then acting Director of the FBI. During those meetings, McCabe alleges in the leaked memos, Rosenstein made comments about invoking the 25th Amendment and wearing a wire when speaking with President Donald Trump.

The next day, Rosenstein signed an order appointing Robert Mueller as a special counsel to investigate Russian interference in the 2016 election. This removed the investigation from the FBI and the influence of McCabe, a man extremely unpopular with Trump and the White House.

Rosenstein has denied that he ever pursued or authorized recording or removing the president. One Justice Department official claimed that Rosenstein's exact comment, made in the midst of an argument with McCabe, was, "Well, what do you want me to do, Andy, wear a wire?"

This is obvious sarcasm, and one would hope that Trump, of all people, would be willing to overlook even the most unfortunate comments made in what the participants thought was a private setting.

Firing Rosenstein would endanger Mueller
In this case, there is plenty of reasons to do so.

Rosenstein was a U.S. attorney under Presidents George W. Bush and Barack Obama, and the Senate confirmed him 94-6 as deputy attorney general. He has been a stellar public servant and a steady, meticulous and ethical second-in-command for Attorney General Jeff Sessions.

It's true Rosenstein has infuriated Trump by his refusal to interfere with Mueller's investigation — but this is a feature, not a bug. It is thoroughly inappropriate for the White House to interfere with an ongoing criminal investigation, and Rosenstein has been completely correct to resist Trump's efforts to do so.

There's another reason to keep Rosenstein at his post. Firing him would cause absolute chaos.

First, it is unclear who would assume control of the Russia investigation. Normally, the solicitor general would assume Rosenstein's duties until a new deputy attorney general can be confirmed. But the current solicitor general, Noel Francisco, has his own potential conflict. The law firm at which he worked, Jones Day, represented the Trump campaign, and his friend and partner, Don McGahn, is White House counsel.

It is more likely that Trump would invoke The Vacancies Act, which gives the president wide discretion to appoint an officer to a position in an "acting capacity" for up to 420 days even though that position normally requires Senate confirmation.

Usually, the "first assistant" to the vacant office takes over. But the president may also appoint any other officer — even one from another department — who has already been confirmed by the Senate. This is what Trump did when he installed Robert Wilkie, an undersecretary at the Department of Defense, as acting secretary of the Department of Veterans Affairs.

The president can also appoint any senior executive already working at the agency in question — in this case, the Justice Department. Rosenstein would have to be replaced by another lawyer, but there are thousands at Justice.

The problem is that Trump has disqualified himself from making such an appointment. He has repeatedly demanded that Sessions and Rosenstein shut down Mueller's investigation. He calls it a "witch hunt" — despite dozens of indictments and even several convictions — and has claimed that the whole idea of Russian interference in the 2016 election is a "hoax" intended only to make him look bad.

Worse, Trump has attacked the attorney general for prosecuting "popular" Republicans because those prosecutions might affect the Republican Party's chances in the midterm elections. Trump clearly doesn't understand that the Justice Department cannot be employed for his political benefit.

Normally, the Senate confirmation process would provide a check on his power to install unfit appointees in the Justice Department. But using The Vacancies Act, there seems little doubt that among the thousands of potential choices, Trump could find at least one willing to politicize the department and shut down the Mueller investigation.

Congress must protect Rosenstein and Mueller
It is in everyone's interest — not the least that of

Congress — to step up to defend Rosenstein and the rule of law before it's too late. Not only has he done nothing meriting dismissal, firing him would force the very legal and political crisis congressional Republicans have been desperately hoping to avoid.

The best solution is to ensure that Rosenstein remains deputy attorney general. But if he is fired, Congress has the tools to take immediate action. The Senate should pass the Special Counsel Independence and Integrity Act, which ensures that any special counsel appointed by the attorney general could not be removed for political reasons. A Senate committee has already approved the bill on a bipartisan 14-7 vote.

This is a "Profiles in Courage" moment in American history. The Mueller investigation must be protected and if Rosenstein is removed, it will be up to Congress to protect it, regardless of the political cost. The investigation into Russian interference in the 2016 election isn't just about Trump. It's not even mostly about Trump. It's about a very well-documented attack on our democracy that has already resulted in indictments or guilty pleas from 35 people and companies.

Fair and free elections are the basis of the American political experiment. Nothing can be allowed to interfere with them. They must be protected against Russia and, if necessary, the president. Senate Majority Leader Mitch McConnell, House Speaker Paul Ryan, history is watching.

Chris Truax, an appellate lawyer in San Diego, is on the legal advisory board of Republicans for the Rule of Law.

Mob rule? Forget it. The First Amendment is not a license to protest anywhere, anytime.

USA Today, October 15, 2018
By Chris Truax

Free speech and the right to protest are limited by the Constitution and the kind of society we want. Calling out mobs is the right thing to do.

Don Lemon, host of CNN Tonight, had an on-air meltdown last week that culminated in this declaration to his audience:

"In the Constitution, you can protest whenever and wherever you want. It doesn't tell you that you can't do it in a restaurant, that you can't do it on a football field. It doesn't tell you that you can't do it on a cable news show, you can do it wherever you want. To call people mobs because they are exercising their constitutional right is just beyond the pale."

This is largely nonsense, and dangerous nonsense at that. But if a respected journalist like Lemon can be so completely mistaken about how the First Amendment works and the exercise of free speech in a civilized society, then anyone can.

The First Amendment covers a lot of territory, including freedom of religion, freedom of the press, the right to assemble and the right to petition for redress of grievances. But when most people think of the First

Amendment, they think of freedom of speech, which includes the freedom to protest.

No right to protest on private property

But the First Amendment doesn't actually give you the right to free speech, and it certainly doesn't give you the right to protest "whenever and wherever you want." Instead, it prevents the government — and only the government — from interfering with your right to free speech. With a few exceptions, anyone else, including a restaurant, a football team or a cable news network, can act to limit speech any way it likes.

In other words, you have no constitutional right to protest on private property. If you decide to stage a demonstration at a restaurant, the restaurant can ask you to leave and have you arrested for trespassing if you refuse. If you decide to engage in political protests at work, you can be fired. You have a right to speech free from governmental interference, but you do not have a right to free speech on someone else's dime. I am sure that Lemon himself appreciates that CNN is not required to allow guests whom they find offensive or disruptive to use CNN to broadcast their message.

This is not to say that the right to protest can or should be restricted. The framers of the Constitution viewed free speech as a necessary element of a civilized and functional society. As with everything, though, there is a time and a place for it.

Which brings up an even more fundamental question. Just because something is legal — or you can get away with it — does not mean that it is good. We too often forget that freedom comes with responsibility.

A few years ago, there was a guy in San Francisco who dressed up as Elmo from Sesame Street and then shouted obscenities at children. Illegal? No. Evil Elmo was protected by the First Amendment. Something that no civilized person would ever imagine doing? Absolutely.

That was an easy one. I think we can all agree we don't want to live in a society where dressing up as a beloved cartoon character and traumatizing children is considered acceptable behavior. Even if it's a constitutional right.

But do we want to live in a society where anyone can be hounded anytime, anywhere because of his political views? That should be an easy one, too. The answer is no.

Calling out a mob is the right thing to do

There is no question that the group of people who ambushed Sen. Ted Cruz, R-Texas, in a restaurant a few weeks ago qualified as a mob and a mob that meant to intimidate and frighten. And they were proud of it, too: "This is a message to Ted Cruz, Brett Kavanaugh, Donald Trump and the rest of the racist, sexist, transphobic and homophobic right-wing scum. You are not safe. We will find you. We will expose you. We will take from you the peace you have taken from so many others."

This is not the kind of society I want to live in. It is not a civilized society at all. It is a society where extremists on both sides terrorize everyone else into silence, a society where the opposite of free speech prevails.

There is much that is broken in our political system.

Even so, we cannot restore civility and reason through intimidation and fear. Don Lemon was wrong. Calling out a mob, even if it happens to be exercising a constitutional right, is not beyond the pale. In fact, it's the right thing — the only thing — to do.

Chris Truax, an appellate lawyer in San Diego, is on the legal advisory board of Republicans for the Rule of Law.

Trump bears moral responsibility for pipe bombs. Denying it just makes things worse.

USA Today, November 1, 2018

By Chris Truax

Nothing Trump has said is illegal, but not everything legal is wise. His reckless rhetoric is inciting violence from fanatics such as Cesar Sayoc.

Between the attempted bombings of prominent Democrats and the Pittsburgh synagogue shooting, America has had an awful run-up to the midterm elections. And President Donald Trump and his surrogates are making it worse.

There is no question that America's political and social fabric is being badly frayed by the anger on both the left and the right. But rather than viewing this as a problem to be solved, the official line coming from the White House is that no one — certainly not Trump — bears any responsibility for the actions of a few "crazies."

No one, they say, blamed the Democrats for the attack by a Bernie Sanders supporter that severely injured House Majority Whip Steve Scalise. Perhaps not, but Sanders did not tell his supporters that Republicans were treasonous or that members of the news media were "enemies of the people." Sanders never congratulated anyone for physically assaulting someone. Nonetheless, the argument being put forward by even traditionally responsible conservatives such as Hugh Hewitt is that no matter how "enthusiastic" their rhetoric, it is deeply unfair to blame political figures for the acts of their most fanatical and obsessive followers.

History of Trump fans threatening violence
This is profoundly hypocritical. The people now defending Trump's rhetoric are the first people to condemn Muslims who preach contempt for their perceived "enemies" in the West, and they are right to do so. While the vast majority of Muslims will not respond with violence, there is a fanatical fringe that will. But Trump's defenders cannot, then, disavow responsibility when their own fanatics take up arms against the "traitors" and "enemies of the people" whom they themselves have preached against.

Perhaps even more disturbing is the reflexive "whataboutism" that seeks to absolve Trump of responsibility for these attacks by pointing to excesses on the left. What about Rep. Maxine Waters? What about "antifa" far-left militant groups? What about liberal mobs chasing Trump's supporters out of restaurants?

What about them? There is no "crazies" arms race where each side must maintain a balance of unhinged fanatics as part of some political "mutually assured destruction" policy. Unilateral crazy disarmament is perfectly workable. That there are badly behaving people on the other side is no excuse for tolerating them on your own.

But the biggest problem is that Trump and his supporters have a pattern here. Cesar Sayoc, the man charged with the attempted bombing of at least 15 of Trump's "enemies," including CNN and Hillary Clinton, is just the latest in a long line of very disturbing Trump supporters threatening political violence. Even during the election, some of his fans were publicly threatening to stage a coup and shoot Clinton. One ex-member of the House, Joe Walsh, tweeted in 2016: "On November 9th, if Trump loses, I'm grabbing my musket. You in?"

While Sayoc is, no doubt, a very disturbed individual, there are many such people in the world. The rhetoric Trump often uses is intended to excite and motivate. And if you have ever seen one of his rallies, you know just how effective it is. Though most of his supporters would not go as far as any sort of violence, some will. Not only has Trump been warned about this time and time again, he has also seen people at his rallies physically assaulted by the crowd.

Something like the Sayoc episode was completely foreseeable. Despite this, Trump has made no effort to dial back his rhetoric. If anything, he has engaged in even more inflammatory attacks in the run-up to Election Day. I doubt seriously whether Trump actually wanted any sort of political violence. Instead, he was simply indifferent as to whether it occurred.

Trump's moral negligence led to Sayoc's bombs

There is a doctrine in criminal law known as "willful, wanton, reckless murder." With regular murder, you must have the intention to kill. But with willful, wanton, reckless murder, while you do not have the intention to kill, you do something very dangerous without really caring or considering whether someone might get killed. The classic example is someone intentionally firing a gun into a house without knowing whether someone is inside. If you kill someone, you are a murderer, whether you intended to shoot them or not.

This is not to suggest that Trump is somehow legally responsible for what Sayoc has done. The president, like all of us, is protected by the First Amendment, and nothing he has said is or should be illegal. Even so, not everything that is legal is wise, and our moral responsibilities are broader than our legal responsibilities. Both Trump and those who have refused to condemn his excesses are morally responsible when his supporters, even his craziest supporters, act on those excesses.

It is true that there are people behaving horribly on both the left and the right. But neither is an excuse for the other. Even if you're not religious, the Bible has a lot of good, practical advice. For example, it teaches that you should first cast the beam out of your own eye before you try to cast the mote out of your brother's. And that's exactly what we should be doing.

I will leave the task of confronting Waters and antifa to the Democrats. As Republicans, we have quite enough work to do.

Chris Truax, an appellate lawyer in San Diego, is on the legal advisory board of Republicans for the Rule of Law.

Sessions firing marks end of Mueller deniability for Republicans. Which side are we on?

USA Today, November 8, 2018
By Chris Truax

Matthew Whitaker has been named to end Mueller's "witch hunt." But the Russia investigation isn't about Trump, it's about defending our democracy.

President Donald Trump appointed Matthew Whitaker as interim attorney general for one reason.

Whitaker, while a former U.S. Attorney, has had a relatively obscure career. Before Attorney General Jeff Sessions appointed him as his chief of staff, he spent several years not practicing law but running a foundation dedicated to publicizing misdeeds —and alleged misdeeds — committed by Hillary Clinton, Elizabeth Warren, Harry Reid and other Democrats.

But there is one thing that really made Whitaker stand out for Trump: his public attacks on special counsel Robert Mueller's investigation, including suggestions on how it might best be sabotaged. Whitaker even suggested that a "stage-crafty" solution to Trump's Mueller problem would be to "reduce his budget to so low that his investigations grind to almost a halt."

Of course, Russian meddling in the 2016 election is not a hoax. Mueller's investigation has already resulted in at least 35 indictments or guilty pleas directly related to active Russian election interference. And it is imperative

51

that Mueller be allowed to complete his investigation which — despite Trump's insistence otherwise — is not all about Donald Trump but, instead, about defending our democracy from those who are actively seeking to destroy it.

Whitaker was chosen to end Mueller 'witch hunt'

So it is beyond question that Matthew Whitaker is not the correct person to oversee Robert Mueller. He has not been appointed so that he can impartially supervise the investigation. He is there to do the president's bidding and end the "witch hunt."

It is very wrong that we should be having this conversation at all. In America, law enforcement should not depend on the whims of one person. We should be relying on our laws and institutions to defend our democracy, not the president's good will. Fortunately, there is a solution ready and waiting to be voted on.

The Senate should pass the Special Counsel Independence and Integrity Act, which provides a measure of protection for Mueller's investigation and ensures that he cannot be removed for political reasons. A Senate committee has already approved the bill on a bipartisan 14-7 vote.

Apart from protecting the current investigation into Russian election meddling, the act makes a lot of sense in general. A special counsel can only be appointed when the Department of Justice itself has a conflict of interest. It seems only reasonable that some checks and balances be in place to ensure that the Justice official supervising the special counsel, whoever it is, cannot remove the special counsel without cause.

While the bill has been reported out of committee,

Senate Majority Leader Mitch McConnell has refused to bring it to the Senate floor for a vote because he believes Trump would not sign it. Perhaps not, but that's what veto overrides are for. For anyone counting at home, the Special Counsel Independence and Integrity Act was passed out of committee with a two-thirds majority, which is exactly the majority needed to override a presidential veto.

McConnell has also refused to let the full Senate vote on the bill protecting the investigation because, he has said, "There's no indication that Mueller's going to be fired." Well, Senator McConnell, there is now.

Republicans are at the end of deniability

It seems that the day of reckoning has come. Trump has made no effort to hide his loathing of the Mueller investigation. He even repeated his attacks at his news conference Wednesday morning. He has now fired Sessions entirely because Sessions followed the law and refused to interfere with that investigation. In his place, he has appointed someone who thinks the investigation should be shut down. Trump's and Whitaker's intentions could not be more clear if they had declared them on Twitter — which they very well might.

As a Republican, I am not in favor of replacing our elephant mascot with an ostrich. We have now come to the end of deniability. There is no question that Whitaker has been appointed specifically to terminate or throttle the Mueller investigation. So the question for our congressional leadership is this: Which side are you on? Will you stand up for our institutions and defend our democracy? Or do you believe that defending Trump is more important?

The base may judge you harshly if you defy Trump and defend the Mueller investigation by passing the Special Counsel Independence and Integrity Act. But history will judge you more harshly still if you do not.

Chris Truax, an appellate lawyer in San Diego, is on the legal advisory board of Republicans for the Rule of Law.

Let Mueller's results speak for themselves

USA Today, November 27, 2018
By Chris Truax

President Donald Trump took to Twitter early Tuesday morning to criticize special counsel Robert Mueller and his investigation, calling Mueller "conflicted" and a "damage to our criminal justice system," marking more than 10 times since the midterm elections that the president has used Twitter to complain about the investigation.

Americans have become familiar with the "witch hunt" narrative, but the president is moving past that ploy by attacking Mueller's character and career, a move not based on facts but on Trump's personal prejudices. Everyone familiar with Mueller's career knows he is a man of integrity and honor who has earned the public's trust.

But support for Mueller should not only reflect his past accomplishments. The success of his investigation is also a key factor. Tuesday's tweets were not the first time the president accused the special counsel of being conflicted, but Trump has yet to provide any evidence for his claim.

While Trump characterizes Mueller's team as "angry Dems," that is both untrue and unworthy. The Justice Department, including Mueller, cannot and does not consider party affiliation when making assignments. Partisan politics have no place in our justice system, and the fact that Trump does not understand this reflects on him rather than the Justice Department.

But the proof is in the pudding. Mueller's results make it clear that his investigation is anything but a partisan ploy. His investigation has indicted or yielded guilty pleas from 32 people and three companies, including two dozen Russians. If that's a witch hunt, Mueller sure is catching a lot of witches.

Most recently, former Trump campaign Chairman Paul Manafort, who was convicted of fraud in August and pleaded guilty to more counts, reneged on his agreement to cooperate with investigators by, Mueller's team alleges, feeding them false information. Other Trump associates who have pleaded guilty to lying to investigators include Rick Gates, Michael Flynn, George Papadopoulos and Alex van der Zwaan. It's hard to see how Mueller's the one who comes out looking untrustworthy.

According to a new poll from Law Works and Hart Research, 82 percent of voters, including 66 percent of Republicans, believe that "Mueller should be allowed to finish his investigation and follow the facts wherever they lead, because everyone must abide by the rule of law, even the president."

So why does the president think Mueller has lost credibility?

Mueller embodies the core values of the American

justice system: prudence, honor and integrity. Mueller is a decorated veteran who has dedicated his life to defending the country from all manner of threats, from foreign armies to terrorists to organized crime. For his courageous and selfless sacrifice and service, the special counsel deserves our trust. Let him do his job. And let his results speak for themselves.

Chris Truax is a practicing attorney and a legal adviser for Republicans for the Rule of Law.

A web of lies and deceit: The Trump-Russia plot thickens with Michael Cohen guilty plea

USA Today, November 29, 2018
By Chris Truax

No apparent smoking gun, yet, on the Trump campaign working with the Russians to win in 2016. But there is one showing collusion on lying to Congress.

Michael Cohen, Donald Trump's personal lawyer, lied to two Republican congressional committees, and Donald Trump is OK with that.

Cohen pleaded guilty Thursday to lying to Congress regarding Trump's involvement in the now infamous efforts to build a Trump Tower in Moscow. Cohen told Congress last year that the efforts ended in early 2016. In fact, court documents show, they continued nearly until the Republican convention.

Cohen originally claimed that the deal died when, in January of 2016, he sent an email about the project to Russian President Vladimir Putin's press secretary, Dmitry Peskov, and never received a response. Not only did Cohen receive a response, he had a 20-minute phone call with an assistant to Peskov ("Russian official 1"). The contacts continued and, that May, Cohen was even invited to "Russia's Davos" along with a possible opportunity to meet either with the prime minister of Russia, Dmitry Medvedev, or with Putin himself.

Coincidentally, the deal was not actually killed off until June 14, 2016, the day The Washington Post broke the story that the Russians had hacked the Democratic National Committee. Huh. Go figure.

Collusion with Russia on lying to Congress
President Trump's response to all this was typically combative, and that's a very bad sign for Trump. We have more than enough data now to conclude that his derision for special counsel Robert Mueller's Russia probe is directly related to it effectiveness. The better Mueller does his job, the louder are the president's claims that it's a waste of money and an "illegal Joseph McCarthy-style witch hunt."
And that's an odd claim coming from Trump, since Roy Cohn, his personal lawyer for many years, was Joe McCarthy's right-hand man during the infamous McCarthy hearings.

What can we make of all this? First, while maybe there isn't a smoking gun, yet, on the Trump campaign working with the Russians to help Trump win the election, there is now a smoking gun proving that the Russians colluded with Trump and his people to lie to Congress.

That is because in August 2017, after Cohen told Congress that he had never heard back from Peskov, the press secretary issued a public statement admitting he had received an email from Cohen and backing Cohen's claim that he never responded: "Since, I repeat again, we do not react to such business topics — this is not our work — we left it unanswered."
Second, President Trump was in this whole mess up to his eyeballs. He made brief remarks to reporters Thursday during which he revealed that he, himself, had

killed off the Moscow deal. "I decided not to do it," he said.

This is directly contrary to what Michael Cohen told Congress when he claimed that he had let the deal lapse in January of 2016 without discussing it with Trump, since he could not move it forward. Who decided to terminate further discussions about the deal with Moscow? It was Trump in June, not Cohen in January.

But Trump knew all this perfectly well when Cohen lied to Congress on his behalf in August of 2017. And yet, he did nothing to correct the record, content to let the lie stand. Perhaps worse, he was perfectly comfortable with the Russian government's complicity in reinforcing it.

Impeachable if Congress wants it to be

Let me make this clear: On Donald Trump's behalf, Michael Cohen and the Russians lied to two Republican-led congressional committees with the specific intent of derailing the Mueller investigation. Trump knew all about this and, at a minimum, did absolutely nothing to stop it or to correct the record. And none of this would ever have come to light were it not for Mueller's dogged efforts to expose the truth and protect our democratic institutions.

Is this impeachable? I don't know. As a practical matter, "high crimes and misdemeanors" are whatever Congress decides they are. But Trump's cynical lies make the very people he claims to lead look like utter fools. By endorsing Cohen's perjury, Trump could not make his contempt for Congress and the Republican majority more clear.

Hopefully that, if nothing else, will finally make congressional Republicans step up and do their jobs by protecting Mueller's investigation. Even lap dogs will bite if you twist their tails.

Chris Truax, an appellate lawyer in San Diego, is on the legal advisory board of Republicans for the Rule of Law.

Trump-Mueller showdown will be a historic test of America's institutions and rule of law

USA Today, December 10, 2018
By Chris Truax

If Justice Department guidelines allowed it, there's no doubt Mueller would have already indicted Trump. The net is closing in now on family and associates.

Special counsel Robert Mueller is showing his hand.

It started Tuesday night, when he filed a memo for Michael's Flynn's long-delayed sentencing after he pleaded guilty on Dec. 1, 2017, to lying to the FBI about his contacts with the Russians during the Trump campaign transition. Mueller recommended that Flynn receive little or no jail time based on his "substantial assistance" to the special counsel investigation.

That assistance seems to have been substantial indeed. Over the course of the past year, Flynn met with Mueller's team or Justice Department attorneys no fewer than 19 times. Fully half of the memo detailing Flynn's assistance is redacted, a reminder that Mueller has a great many lines of investigation that no one, not even President Donald Trump, knows anything about.

Then Mueller filed sentencing memos for Paul Manafort and Michael Cohen. While Flynn got full credit for his early acceptance of responsibility and his complete cooperation, Manafort had his cooperation agreement rescinded because he was apparently incapable of being truthful. Not only has he lost the opportunity for his sentence to be reduced, Mueller will be asking the court to impose an even longer sentence because of Manafort's false statements.

Mueller's memo details multiple instances of Manafort telling seemingly pointless lies about things that Mueller already knew about. When confronted, he'd eventually tell the truth, only to then tell yet another lie. While some parts of the memo are redacted, many of the lies Manafort told had to do with his relationship with Konstantin Kilimnik, a Russian-Ukrainian political consultant who is also likely a Russian intelligence operative.

Where does this leave President Donald Trump?

Mueller's sentencing memo in Cohen's case was, in many ways, the most interesting and certainly the most humorous. If Flynn got an A and Manafort got an F, Mueller gave Cohen a B-. Mueller recommended that Cohen receive a substantial prison sentence but because of his "useful" cooperation, Mueller recommended that Cohen be sentenced to something less than the42 months recommended by the Probation Department. The special counsel also recommended that Cohen serve the sentences for his existing cases concurrently, a potentially big break for Cohen. All in all, Cohen will probably end up serving a sentence of 24 to 36 months.

Cohen did not receive full credit for cooperation because he did not fully cooperate. While he was apparently very forthcoming regarding his relationship with Trump and the Trump Organization, he was less so regarding his own separate criminal activity. Much to the Mueller team's apparent annoyance, Cohen continued to minimize and even misrepresent his culpability for bank fraud and tax evasion. Cohen also declined to "come clean" about possible uncharged criminal conduct, a necessary step for being considered an actual "cooperating witness" in the Southern District of New York.

Of course, the question in everyone's mind, including Donald Trump's, is, "Where does that leave Donald Trump?" The answer to that still isn't clear but, with these sentencing memos, it's now starting to come into focus.

First, the comedy. The New York prosecutors' Cohen memo contains the memorable line, "On approximately June 16, 2015, Individual-1, for whom Cohen worked at the time, began an ultimately successful campaign for President of the United States."

The memo goes on to charge "Individual-1" with conspiracy to commit the same felony campaign finance violations that Cohen pleaded guilty to. There appears to be no question whatsoever that if Justice Department guidelines allowed it, Mueller would have already indicted Trump.

Apparently, though, Mueller was just too cryptic for the president who, after Cohen's sentencing memo was released, tweeted out, "Totally clears the President. Thank you!"

Now, the tragedy, at least if you are a member of Donald Trump's inner circle: The net is closing in. The most interesting thing in the sentencing memo was Mueller revealing that the conspiracy to violate campaign finance laws was not just limited to "Individual-1" and Cohen. "Executives" of The Trump Organization (called "the company" in the memo) concocted a scheme to reimburse Cohen for his illegal campaign contributions without revealing that they were campaign-related.

It isn't clear from the memo who the "executives" are, but there is a very small pool of candidates and most of them are members of the Trump family. One or more of them is almost certain to be indicted.

Trump will test our institutions and rule of law

Finally, Mueller chose to drop yet another bombshell in his Cohen memo. "Fourth, Cohen described the circumstances of preparing and circulating his response to the congressional inquiries, while continuing to accept responsibility for the false statements contained within it."

What Mueller is saying here is that Cohen's lies to Congress weren't just Cohen's idea. It has been obvious since Cohen's guilty plea that Trump knew Cohen had lied to Congress and did nothing to correct the record. Now it appears that at least some people in Trump's inner circle knew in advance that Cohen would lie and even helped him do it.

Difficult and dangerous times are ahead. There is now no chance that Mueller's investigation will end with a whimper, or that a detailed report will be smothered by an attorney general keen to protect the president. At the very least, there is an indictment waiting for "Individual-1" whenever his presidency ends. And in the near term, there is almost certainly an indictment in the works for one of Trump's inner circle, possibly even a member of his family. And this is based only on what Mueller did not black out in the memos.

Trump is unlikely to accept any of this. The coming clash will test our institutions and the rule of law as never before. But whether they emerge from this clash irreparably damaged or newly invigorated isn't up to Trump or Mueller. It's up to you.

Speak up. Write a letter to the editor. Call your representative. Call your senator. America's institutions aren't going to defend themselves. That's our job.

Chris Truax, an appellate lawyer in San Diego, is on the legal advisory board of Republicans for the Rule of Law.

Dear Democrats, please forgo progressive payback in 2020. We just need to land the plane.

USA Today, December 31, 2018
By Chris Truax

It's tempting for progressive Democrats to view 2020 as an opportunity to remake America in their own image. As an American, I beg you not to do this.

On Jan. 15, 2009, US Airways Flight 1549 lost power in both engines while taking off from New York's La Guardia Airport. Unable to restart either engine and lacking enough altitude to make the turn back to the airport, the pilot, Captain Chesley Sullenberger, chose to attempt an unprecedented water landing in the Hudson River. In what came to be known as "The Miracle on the Hudson," Sully managed to safely ditch the plane and all 155 passengers and crew were saved.

In 2020, America is facing its own Flight 1549 election. We don't need a pilot who will take us higher, faster and farther then ever before. We don't need a pilot who will make America do barrel rolls and loop-the-loops. We need a pilot who can land the damn plane.

Progressives often get annoyed when well-meaning conservatives offer them political advice. So I am not going to do that. Instead, I am speaking to you as one American to another about what our country needs.

It is tempting for progressive Democrats to view 2020

as their big opportunity to remake America in their own image. All we have to do, the thinking goes, is find a candidate who can win 51% of the vote. Since Trump will be wildly unpopular, that candidate can be very, very progressive indeed. Given the choice between a Democratic Socialist and four more years of Donald Trump, even Mitt Romney might hold his nose and vote Democratic!

As an American, I beg you not to do this. First, you can all too easily miscalculate. Hillary Clinton got 4 percent more votes than Donald Trump and look what happened to her.

But even worse, you might be successful. If we have learned anything over the last 10 years, it's that big changes need broad buy-in. Even when you have all the power, forcing through your agenda over the objections and down the throats of the other side results in a Pyrrhic victory at best.

America needs calm and retrenchment
When Democrats finally managed to pass Obamacare on a straight party-line vote back in 2010, they thought the hard work was done and the matter settled. How wrong they were. The passage of Obamacare over uniform Republican opposition became a permanent rallying cry for the right and has been a prominent issue in the last five elections as well as a source of more-or-less constant legislative action. Since its passage, Congress has made more than sixty efforts to repeal it.

Now, Republicans have created their own "Obamacare." Just as Obamacare was for Republicans,

Justice Brett Kavanaugh will be for Democrats. There will be investigations, efforts to alter the composition of the Supreme Court and the terms of the Justices, even impeachment proceedings. And the fight will go on and on and on . . .

America does not need any more permanent political canker sores and, as a fellow American, I beg you not to create any. But if Democrats attempt to install an extremely progressive president in the White House with an agenda of turning America into a democratic-socialist City on the Hill, that is exactly what you will be doing. The 49% of the country that did not vote Democratic will be infuriated and threatened. And a Donald Trump 2.0 will arise to channel that fear and anger for 2024. And the fight will go on and on and on . . .

What America needs is a period of calm and retrenchment. A period to bind up our wounds and to begin again to view our fellow Americans as decent people who respect each other's concerns even when they disagree with them and who want what is best for America rather than their party. What America needs is a steady — and trusted — hand on the tiller. Someone with the wisdom to recognize America's problems but with the humility to find consensus in solving them. What we need is someone to land the damn plane.

Steady, calm hands, not progressive payback
I can think of several Democrats who could play this role. Personally, I could do with four years of Joe Biden. But there are many Democrats — quite a few of them likely presidential candidates — who do not fit this

description at all. Rather than seeking to land the plane, they are the candidates of progressive payback.

Please, for my sake, for America's sake, please do not nominate such a candidate in 2020, even though someone like this might well win the presidency. I ask you for your restraint and your forbearance.

It is true, I admit, that the most partisan Republicans will not thank you no matter what you do. In the current political climate, I am sure that someone will send out a scathing tweet about the next president's Thanksgiving proclamation. But most Americans will thank you, conservative and liberal alike. And even the most partisan will recognize that you chose healing over revenge, even if they will not admit it.

The American political system has been spiraling downward for a number of years now. Someone has to be big enough and wise enough to call a halt to this cycle of destruction and start rebuilding our trust in our institutions and our trust in each other. Sadly, I doubt that it will be my party. Will it be yours?

Chris Truax, a Republican, is an appellate lawyer in San Diego.

Trump's 'border security' shutdown: Cut off cash to people and agencies that protect us

USA Today January 3, 2019
By Chris Truax

In the name of strengthening border security, Trump refuses to fund the FBI, TSA, Coast Guard and Border Patrol(!). You can't make this stuff up.

With the government shutdown now in its second week, President Donald Trump has doubled down on his demand for a border wall. As Trump explained, "We need Border Security, and as EVERYONE knows, you can't have Border Security without a Wall. The Drones & Technology are just bells and whistles." He's even threatened to shut down the border entirely and close America's ports of entry with Mexico if his demands aren't met.

But there is a problem with Trump's steely-eyed determination to keep the government partially shut down in the name of border security. There is no polite way to put this, but facts are facts and there is no room for debate: If the president really wants to protect our borders, this shutdown is objectively stupid, no ifs, ands or buts.

Only about a quarter of the government is actually feeling the impact of the shutdown because Trump refuses to sign a continuing resolution to keep that portion funded. But the affected agencies include the FBI, which works tirelessly to keep this country safe from terrorist attacks, along with the Coast Guard, the

Border Patrol(!) and the Transportation Security Administration. All this in the name of strengthening border security. You couldn't make this stuff up.

Many of the employees at these agencies perform what are considered "essential services" so instead of being ordered to stay home, they must continue working. But they aren't getting paychecks. Federal employees take their missions seriously and the vast majority of them will continuing doing their best. But even so, the toll of not receiving paychecks will wear on them just as it would any of us.

Some of the most critical federal employees are also the lowest paid. About half of TSA screeners, for example, make less than $40,000 a year. It is already tremendously difficult to keep TSA screeners on the job and the federal government employs over 40,000 of them. At some airports, the annual turnover rate for screeners is 80 percent. And this shutdown is only going to make things worse.

Top Trump concern is securing base, not border
How many paychecks do you think TSA screeners can miss before they are forced to find another job — any job — to pay the bills? When they do leave, commercial aviation will start to grind to a halt. Worse, there will be no money to hire or train their replacements. So even after Trump decides to fund the TSA again, it will be weeks — perhaps months — before the security lines are fully staffed again and airlines can resume their normal schedules.

This isn't governing. It's rampant silliness. There is not

a single person who actually thinks that forcing Border Patrol agents work without pay, or driving them to find new jobs, will somehow increase border security. So why has Trump painted himself into this corner?

I'm afraid that the answer is that Trump actually does not care about border security at all. It's been obvious for quite some time that the main thing Donald Trump likes about being president is holding rallies. What he cares about is his "base" — specifically, the people who are willing to show up and cheer for him.

Our president loves his "Build the wall!" chants. Nothing would cause him greater pain that standing on a stage in front of 10,000 of his erstwhile supporters and being booed instead of cheered. Before the shutdown, Trump had made clear that he was willing to sign a bill to keep the government open, even if it did not include funding for his wall. Because of Trump's support, the Senate unanimously passed such a funding bill. But then his "base," in the form of various pundits and talk-show hosts, began demanding that Trump shut down the government instead of signing a bill that did not include wall money. Rather than face their scorn, Trump reversed his position.

Trump doesn't really care about the wall any more than he cares about border security. All he really cares about is being seen to fight for the wall so that people will continue cheering him at his rallies.

GOP should let Trump go down fighting
This is no way to run a country. I am sure that Democrats are tempted to stand by and watch Trump

destroy everything he claims to care about until even his staunchest congressional supporters are willing to accept any deal that will end the chaos. Nonetheless, Democrats are advancing plans to immediately reopen the government and get these agencies funded again.

The question is, how will Republicans respond? Many House and Senate Republicans are claiming they will hold the line and refuse to reopen the government until Trump gets what he wants. While this makes a good sound bite, it is both irresponsible and unsustainable. No possible political interest can justify courting Border Patrol departures and maybe even a strike, or watching the commercial aviation system strained to the verge of collapse.

The kindest thing Republicans can do is to let Trump go down fighting. They should back the Democrats' efforts to reopen the government and, if necessary, vote to override Trump's veto. This will straighten out the current mess while allowing Trump to claim he did everything he possibly could to keep faith with his fans but was stabbed in the back by "traitorous" Republicans.

This is a small price to pay for getting cash flowing once again into agencies like the FBI and the Border Patrol that really do protect America. And being a "traitor" to Donald Trump is far preferable to being a traitor to common sense and the public good.

It will also finally create a consensus that there are limits to what will be tolerated from President Trump. You wouldn't think agreeing that defunding the Border

Patrol is not the way you increase border security would be a major breakthrough in bipartisanship, but we've got to start somewhere.

Chris Truax, a Republican, is an appellate lawyer in San Diego.

Donald Trump's government shutdown cripples FBI, raises terrorism risk

USA Today, January 24, 2019
By Chris Truax

If terrorists attack us during this shutdown because of a weakened FBI, the buck will stop with Donald Trump and America will never forgive him.
Now, it's getting real.

We know what the shutdown is doing to airport security and of the growing inability of Transportation Security Administration agents to even afford to get to work. The consequences for air travel are obvious. Sooner or later, if the shutdown continues, commercial aviation will grind to a halt.

FBI agents have been suffering more silently, but more severely. Until this week. On Tuesday, the FBI Agents Association released a 72-page report outlining some of the unclassified ways that the shutdown has made it difficult or impossible for them to do their jobs. We can only guess at the problems the FBI is having that cannot be publicly disclosed.

The report makes for some chilling reading. The FBI's counterterrorism activities are suffering badly. One agent quoted in the report warns, "The shutdown has eliminated any ability to operate. ... It's bad enough to work without pay, but we can only conduct administrative functions while doing it. The fear is our enemies know they can run freely."

To take one example, the FBI maintains an extensive network of sensitive sources to monitor terrorist threats from around the world. But due to the shutdown, they aren't able to pay them: "We have lost several sources who have worked for months, and years, to penetrate groups and target subjects. These assets cannot be replaced."

Even worse, in some cases, FBI agents aren't even able to contact their informants: "I am unable to buy the phone card that I use to recharge my 'cold' phone ... to talk to a very valuable (confidential human source who) reports on domestic and international terrorism."

Agents are scrounging for tires, office supplies
Even the physical assets being used by the FBI are being exhausted or simply breaking down. The situation is so bad that agents have been reduced to cannibalizing equipment: "We are out of tires. Our mechanics are cannibalizing out-of-service vehicles in an effort to replace flat tires. … We are almost out of copy paper. … Supplies needed for forensic processing are being expended and not being replaced. We are now almost out of trace evidence filters, casting material, DNA swab kits, etc., with no ability to replenish them."

Investigations are being shelved because the FBI is unable to afford to go to court to get grand jury subpoenas. This, however, soon won't matter because the court system itself has been defunded. It has been running on fumes since the shutdown in a heroic effort to keep the courthouse doors open but, eventually, those efforts will fail and the courts will close. This means no subpoenas, no grand juries, no indictments and no trials. Come to think of it, it's probably a good thing, because there is also no money to run federal prisons or pay prison staff, including the guards.

There is an irrefutable, unshakable point here, and it has nothing to do with politics: When it comes to defending America, especially against international terrorism, the buck stops with the president.

Trump is failing to protect and defend us

This is a mantle that every president, regardless of party, has understood and freely accepted. You may disagree with what President George W. Bush or President Barack Obama did, maybe you think they went too far, maybe you think they didn't go far enough. But there is no denying that keeping America safe from terrorism was their highest priority. And they knew that if something did go wrong on their watch, they would be held accountable for it.

Mr. President, go ahead and shut down the TSA if you want. If you believe that building your wall is worth the political heat you would get for crippling America's civil aviation system and making it impossible to fly, that's your call.

But what you cannot do is open America up to a terrorist attack to advance your political agenda. Making sure the FBI has the resources it needs to protect America is your job. Not House Speaker Nancy Pelosi's. Not Senate Majority Leader Mitch

McConnell's. Your job. And you are failing in it. And if, because of your failure, America is attacked, there will be no excuses, no shifting of blame. It will be your responsibility. And America will never, ever forgive you.

So do your job, Mr. President. Get funds flowing again to the FBI. If you do not, America — and you — will suffer the consequences.

Chris Truax, an appellate lawyer in San Diego, is on the legal advisory board of Republicans for the Rule of Law.

Donald Trump's emergency declaration is an attack on democracy

USA Today, February 15, 2019
By Chris Truax

Invoking a bogus emergency to build a wall Congress rejected will have long-term impacts on the rule of law.
President Donald Trump has officially declared an "emergency" on the southern border so that he can build his wall.

I won't go into all the reasons why this emergency is bogus or why, even after declaring an emergency, he still won't be able to build his wall. Instead, I want to discuss why willfully damaging our democratic institutions for a little short-term political gain is a very bad, very un-American, idea.

If there is any emergency at all here, it's a political one. Trump felt no pressing need for the wall for the past two years, and nothing of emergency proportions on the ground has changed. What has changed is control of the House of Representatives. When Republicans lost their unified control of Congress, Trump lost any chance whatsoever of fulfilling his "Build the wall!" promise that his base loves so much.

The "emergency" here is that Trump isn't able to get Congress to agree to what he wants. If he's unable to build his wall, even his most dedicated fans will turn on him. That may seem like an emergency to Trump, but it certainly isn't the kind of thing that could, even theoretically, justify making an end run around Congress. People booing Trump at his rallies is not the equivalent of the zombie apocalypse.

The old saying that what goes around comes around is nowhere more true than in politics. The reason that Trump and the Republican Senate have been confirming very conservative judges at a breakneck pace isn't down to Senate Majority Leaders Mitch McConnell's political savvy. It's because Harry Reid, the former Senate majority leader, decided to eliminate the filibuster for judicial nominations so that it would be easier for Democrats to confirm more liberal judges. How's that working for you, Harry?

Trump's declaration of an "emergency" on the southern border is exactly the same thing. Someday, Democrats will control the presidency and won't be able to get, say, a Republican Senate to take action on one of their pet issues. If Trump can declare an emergency to expropriate land and build his wall, some future president will be able to declare an emergency to shut coal mines and build windmills.

Nor is this threat fanciful. Numerous Democrats, including House Speaker Nancy Pelosi herself, have made the warning — or perhaps, threat — explicit. Rep. Emanuel Cleaver of Missouri tweeted, "Gun violence is a national emergency. Climate change is a national emergency. Income inequality is a national emergency. Access to health care is a national emergency. Building a wall on the southern border is not."

Circumventing congress

None of these things is even a remotely acceptable reason for attempting to circumvent our constitutional system of government and the ordinary legislative process. And I think it is safe to say every Republican in Congress would be violently opposed to any effort by a Democrat to do so. But sauce for the goose is sauce for the gander, and if Republicans are unwilling to oppose Trump declaring an emergency because he is unable to get Congress to pass the legislation he wants, they won't be able to object when President Bernie Sanders does the same thing.

Our democratic institutions are far more important than whatever the issue of the day happens to be. Two decades from now, no one will remember whatever it is that seems so important to us today. But our institutions endure and if we damage them, everyone will remember what we have done, whether 20 years from now or a hundred. There is nothing that can justify opening the door — even a crack — to the idea that a president is entitled to rule by decree when politics and our constitutional system of government become inconvenient.

Fortunately, Congress will have an opportunity to reject Trump's declaration. The National Emergencies Act allows Congress to pass a joint resolution overturning an emergency declaration. If the president vetoes the resolution, both houses of Congress would have to vote to overturn his veto by a two-thirds majority to terminate the emergency. This is a steep hill to climb but not an impossible one, especially when there is so much at stake.

Declaring an emergency in the absence of one is an affront to our constitutional system of government and the rule of law itself. Our southern border isn't facing an emergency, but our democratic institutions are. No president should ever be allowed to invoke "emergency" powers simply because he can't get what he wants through the normal political process. That is a gross abuse of the office of the presidency and sets a dangerous precedent for future presidential administrations.

Every American, regardless of party, should oppose it. Congressional Republicans, in particular, need to stand up to President Trump and block this emergency declaration. If they do not, they will have no one to blame but themselves for what comes next.

Chris Truax, an appellate lawyer in San Diego, is on the legal advisory board of Republicans for the Rule of Law.

Skimpy Barr letter sets up constitutional battle royal to force full Mueller report release

USA Today, March 24, 2019
By Chris Truax

I can absolutely guarantee the House is going to demand to see every single comma of the obstruction section. Barr's conclusion isn't good enough.

I am not a fan of Donald Trump but I am happy — almost ecstatic — to report that the president is not a Russian agent. That's the good news in Attorney General William Barr's four-page letter to Congress about special counsel Robert Mueller's report.

Unfortunately, the letter makes clear that the Russians considered Trump to be what used to be known as a "useful idiot," someone who would unknowingly advance Russian interests with no need for any sort of direct control.

Barr's letter confirms again that the Russians were all in for Trump and were actively involved in influencing the 2016 election in his favor. These efforts included, among other things, hacking various computers and widely distributing stolen e-mails that would damage the Clinton campaign. The special counsel found that the campaign and its associates had not "coordinated or conspired with the Russian government in these efforts" despite multiple offers of help from "Russian-affiliated individuals."

Less reassuring is how the Mueller report deals with whether or not Trump is guilty of obstruction of justice. Mueller decided to punt and, rather than draw his own conclusion, he laid out the evidence and invited the attorney general to make the final call. Barr, in his letter, said he concluded the evidence was insufficient to establish that the president committed "an obstruction of justice offense."

This, I'm afraid, is where we are going to have a problem. I can absolutely guarantee that Congress, especially the House, is going to demand to see every single comma of at least this section of the report. Barr's conclusion simply isn't good enough. Especially when, somewhat disturbingly, Barr observes that "many of (Trump's actions) took place in public view." This, of course, raises the question of what actions took place out of public view that we don't know about yet.

A constitutional battle is coming
In the coming months, there is going to be a constitutional battle royal over making the report, especially this section, public. The attorney general, as he must, will not voluntarily release portions of the report that are required to remain confidential under "applicable law, regulations and Departmental policies." Barr is also very intent on scrubbing information from the report that has been obtained through a grand jury.

Unlike the attorney general, however, Congress can ignore all of these considerations. Congress is a separate, co-equal branch of government, and both the House and Senate have their own subpoena powers and a constitutionally mandated duty of oversight. If Congress wants to press the issue, its subpoenas cannot be avoided by appeals to Justice Department regulations and policies or even grand jury secrecy. Congress even has an inherent contempt power that would allow the House to order its sergeant at arms to arrest and incarcerate anyone refusing to honor a subpoena issued by a House committee.

This power hasn't been used since 1934, but it's available should Congress decide to flex its muscles. In summary, if Congress decides to fully exercise its subpoena power, there are very limited grounds on which Barr can refuse to produce the full report and even fewer grounds on which Mueller could resist a subpoena commanding him to testify before Congress. Let's all hope it doesn't come to that.

What Barr's letter leaves out is also important
Finally, and perhaps most ominous, there's what Barr's letter doesn't say. He confirms that there are no further indictments pending and that there are no sealed indictments filed. But he also observes that there are "other ongoing matters, including those that the special counsel has referred to other offices." In other words, while Mueller isn't planning on filing any other indictments himself, it doesn't mean that other indictments from other offices aren't still in the works.

This makes a good deal of sense as Mueller had a limited mandate to investigate matters arising out of Russian efforts to influence the 2016 election. We know he has already sought assistance from the Southern District of New York with respect to Michael Cohen; it now appears he has passed off other cases as well. There could well be more to come. At the very least, we know that there are likely potential cases pending against "Individual 1" and other people in the Trump organization for felony campaign finance violations.

So please do not remove your seat belt until the ride has come to a complete stop.

Chris Truax, an appellate lawyer in San Diego, is on the legal advisory board of Republicans for the Rule of Law.

Mueller report redactions: How Congress will make sure we find out everything important

USA Today , April 17, 2019
By Chris Truax

The Mueller report that is released to the public this week will not be the final version, not by a long shot.
Attorney General William Barr has removed four kinds of material from the report. But Congress is a separate branch of government, with its own constitutional duties and powers of investigation. By issuing a formal subpoena, it can bypass many of the laws and regulations that bind the attorney general, and insist on access to much of the information Barr holds back.

Here are the four categories of redacted material and how Congress could get to see them:

▶ Grand jury information. Grand jury proceedings are usually kept secret unless an investigation results in an indictment. But there are several exceptions. The one Congress is most likely to use allows the court to unseal grand jury information "preliminarily to or in connection with a judicial proceeding."

It is well-established that an impeachment proceeding is a "judicial proceeding." And it's hard to argue that a congressional investigation of potential wrongdoing by the president, especially if it's something like obstructing justice or dodgy dealings with Russians, isn't a necessary preliminary to what might become an impeachment proceeding.

There's a very solid precedent for this, courtesy of President Richard Nixon. In Haldeman v. Sirica, the court endorsed exactly this reasoning when it ordered the release of grand jury information to Congress. The House Judiciary Committee reviewed the information privately and used it as a road map for its 1974 impeachment proceedings. It became public only last October.

It's up to a court, not Barr or the Department of Justice, to decide whether secrecy ought to be waived in a particular case. Congress would likely file such an application within a week of receiving the redacted report.

▶ National security. Information that could reveal intelligence sources and methods is the most sensitive category in the report, but it is also the easiest for Congress to access. Congress regularly reviews extremely sensitive intelligence data and there are statutes and procedures in place to allow it to do so. There is even a special exemption allowing this information to be shared with Congress on the list of exceptions to grand jury secrecy.

In the most sensitive cases, the intelligence is shared only with the Gang of Eight — the top Democrats and Republicans (chairs and ranking members) on the House and Senate Intelligence committees, as well as the House and Senate majority and minority leaders. This helps ensure that everything in the Mueller report that should be made public will be made public.

▶ Ongoing criminal investigations. This is where Barr and Congress are most likely to be at loggerheads. While the DOJ has a strong interest in protecting ongoing investigations, Congress has an equally strong interest in seeing the full picture of special counsel Robert Mueller's findings.

There is an element of "hiding the ball" in saying Mueller won't be filing any more indictments, yet redacting large quantities of information regarding criminal investigations that Mueller has passed off to others. Congress may well decide that transparency is more important than the risk of compromising a potential prosecution.

Congress has an absolute right to conduct oversight investigations even if they conflict with a criminal investigation or prosecution. While the DOJ regularly asserts an "ongoing investigation" privilege to protect its own files and records from a congressional subpoena, the extent of that privilege has never been fully determined by a court.

Instead, congressional demands for information that might impact a criminal investigation are virtually always resolved through intense negotiations between DOJ officials and the committee conducting the investigation.

Sometimes the compromise is a confidential briefing. Sometimes Congress agrees to keep the material being turned over confidential. Sometimes the DOJ relents and gives Congress all or part of the information it requested. It will likely work the same way here. The Barr version of the Mueller report isn't the end of a process. It's the opening bid in a negotiation. Expect Congress to eventually have access to a lot more information on other investigations than Barr is currently making available.

▶ Third party privacy rights. DOJ policy is to not reveal information about people who aren't being prosecuted in order to protect their privacy rights. Barr has said he'll be redacting information regarding "peripheral" third parties, and that he will not redact information to protect President Donald Trump's reputation. But these are subjective judgments. If Barr strictly followed the policy, the report would consist of nothing but the indictments Mueller had already filed and, since no charges are being filed, the section on obstruction of justice would be blank.

It's unlikely a court would allow the DOJ to resist a congressional subpoena on the grounds that a third party might find it embarrassing if the information were provided to Congress. While it is true that Congress can't compel the production of evidence without a proper purpose, looking into potential presidential misconduct is about as proper as it gets.

There's even a statute making it clear that potential embarrassment is not a valid reason for refusing to testify before Congress. But, much like concerns about information that might disrupt an ongoing criminal investigation, both Congress and the DOJ have a shared interest in handling this information correctly. So expect this to be another area of negotiation.

Hanging over all this is Congress' inherent power to enforce its own subpoenas. While Congress typically seeks assistance from a court, it doesn't have to. The power hasn't been used since 1934, but Congress can find people (even an attorney general) in contempt, and have them arrested and held until they comply with a congressional subpoena. As one court put it, this would be "an unseemly constitutional confrontation that should be avoided." So let's hope it doesn't come to that.

Finally, there is the question of what additional information the public might eventually see. The short answer is that, under the Speech and Debate clause of the Constitution, congressional committees and even individual legislators have absolute authority to place any information into the Congressional Record that they see fit. In one of the Pentagon Papers cases, Alaska Sen. Mike Gravel read extensively from classified material and then entered more than 4,000 pages of the Pentagon Papers into the record.

As a practical matter, Congress seldom makes use of this privilege and usually respects protections for classified and otherwise sensitive material. But if Congress does discover something in all this redacted material — even highly classified material — that it believes the public needs to know, it will be published. It can't be covered up.

The bottom line: If the unredacted Mueller report is made available for congressional review, we can be confident there will be no hidden smoking gun. That's probably the best single argument for releasing the entire report to Congress, even if it can't be made public.

Chris Truax, an appellate lawyer in San Diego, is on the legal advisory board of Republicans for the Rule of Law.

Mueller report: Attorney General Barr jumped the gun in clearing Trump of obstruction

USA Today, April 18, 2019
By Chris Truax

Contrary to Barr's conclusion, the Mueller report leaves very much open the question of whether President Trump is guilty of obstruction of justice.

Detailed analysis of the redacted Mueller report that was released Thursday will go on for weeks. But one thing is immediately clear: Attorney General William Barr jumped the gun when he declared last month and again Thursday that special counsel Robert Mueller did not find enough evidence to "establish that the President committed an obstruction-of-justice offense."

First, Barr has form here. Long before he was attorney general or knew any of the facts we know now, he had conclusively decided that it would be impossible for Trump to obstruct justice. So it's no surprise that his opinion hasn't changed now that the report is out.

But Mueller and his team came to a different conclusion. While recognizing that "the evidence we obtained about the President's actions and intent presents difficult issues," they did not conclude that the evidence of obstruction was on the fence and decide to leave the final determination to Barr. Instead, they concluded that, despite the evidence they had uncovered, it would be improper to make a formal finding that the president had violated the law. They made this decision not because they concluded the president was not guilty, but because, under current Department of Justice practice, a sitting president can't be indicted.

Mueller's team offered two reasons for declining to recommend prosecution of the president on obstruction charges. First, "a federal criminal accusation against a sitting President would place burdens on the President's capacity to govern and potentially preempt constitutional processes for addressing presidential misconduct." Translation: If we make a formal finding that the president violated the law that might interfere with Congress's impeachment authority.

No ringing endorsement of Trump's innocence
Second, if they did make a decision to prosecute, it would be at least two years and possibly six before the charges could be adjudicated, and that would be unfair to the president personally. "Fairness concerns counseled against potentially reaching that judgment when no charges can be brought.

The ordinary means for an individual to respond to an accusation is through a speedy and public trial . . . In contrast , a prosecutor's judgment that crimes were committed, but that no charges will be brought, affords no such adversarial opportunity for public name-clearing before an impartial adjudicator."

None of this is a ringing endorsement of Trump's innocence. On the contrary. In Mueller's own words, "[I]f we had confidence after a thorough investigation of the facts that the President clearly did not commit obstruction of justice, we would so state. Based on the facts and the applicable legal standards, however, we are unable to reach that judgment."

Impeachment is still on the table

In addition, whether Trump committed an actual federal crime does not completely answer the question we must decide. As the report points out, ultimately, it is up to Congress to sanction a sitting president and that determination is more than just a question of whether the president is an actual felon. For example, one of the reasons Barr believes the president did not commit obstruction is that the president's efforts to interfere with the investigation were not motivated by "corrupt intent." Rather, he said, Trump was personally upset and believed the investigation was "undermining his presidency, propelled by his political opponents, and fueled by illegal leaks."

Assuming that is so and that interfering with an investigation for political reasons doesn't qualify as corrupt intent — a big assumption — that still does not necessarily absolve the president. Even things that fall short of criminality can trigger a congressional investigation or even impeachment proceedings. Whether Trump crossed a line is a call for Congress to make, not Mueller or Barr.

Mueller intended both the American people and Congress to judge the results of his investigation for themselves. That's why he produced a report that, even with redactions, runs to almost 450 pages. Contrary to the attorney general's conclusion, the question of whether Trump is guilty of obstructing justice is still very much open.

Chris Truax, an appellate lawyer in San Diego, is on the legal advisory board of Republicans for the Rule of Law.

How do you solve a problem like Donald Trump? Impeachment isn't the answer. Yet.

USA Today, May 9, 2019
By Chris Truax

The truth is that the president is incredibly inept. Trump doesn't so much represent the banality of evil as he does the evil of banality.

After digesting special counsel Robert Mueller's report and watching Attorney General William Barr's Senate testimony, I've concluded, among other things, that Barr is simply wrong. I'm convinced that a reasonable prosecutor could charge President Donald Trump with obstruction of justice.

But that's something of a red herring. Whether Trump's actions were actually illegal or merely unacceptable is beside the point. The question is, what do we do about it? Should the president be impeached?

That's certainly what some people, outraged by his conduct in office and insisting he must be held to account, are demanding. But I'm far more concerned about minimizing damage to our democratic institutions and our political fabric than I am about punishing anyone.

And impeachment isn't a punishment. Rather, it's the ultimate safeguard protecting those institutions from the worst kinds of malfeasance. Punishment is reserved for criminal law, and the president is answerable for all of his acts once he's out of office, no matter how that occurs.

The real question isn't whether Trump should be punished for obstruction. It's whether impeaching the president is the best way to protect our democracy from further harm. I'm not convinced. It's true there would be an undeniable satisfaction in finally "doing something" to push back against Trump's behavior in office.

But impeachment would also be extremely disruptive and divisive. Worse, it would be little more than a gesture. The House probably would have the votes to impeach (or charge) him. But absent some stunning new revelation, the GOP-run Senate just isn't going muster the two-thirds majority necessary to convict and remove the president. It might not even try the case, a constitutional nightmare all on its own.

A B-list celebrity desperate for attention
I'm also not convinced that Trump "merits" impeachment. Yes, the president has behaved outrageously in office, from attempting to interfere with the Mueller investigation to pressuring the attorney general not to prosecute Republicans. But it's a little bit like when someone living in a memory care facility goes on a shoplifting spree. Everyone can see this is very wrong and that steps must be taken to ensure it never happens again. But it's all kind of sad and maybe isn't best resolved through formal legal channels.

The truth is that the president is incredibly inept.

Trump doesn't so much represent the banality of evil as he does the evil of banality. He continues to behave like a B-list celebrity desperate for attention and with one eye on the judgment of his fans — rather than as the president of the United States with one eye on the judgment of history. He's incapable of understanding the serious responsibilities with which he has been entrusted. The reason he publicly advocates things like politicizing the Justice Department is because he simply doesn't understand why that would be wrong. But this makes him less dangerous to our fundamental institutions rather than more. It's hard to subvert what you don't understand.

So I don't think impeachment is the answer. But we can't just ignore the problem, either. What we — and Congress — need to do is take steps to limit the damage by empowering the people around the president to do their jobs ethically. The message is, "There will be accountability, so mind what you do." People near the president know right from wrong even if Trump does not. Knowing there will be a reckoning, where the faithful will be rewarded and the guilty exposed, will go a long way in helping these people do the right thing.

This means congressional oversight and lots of it. Trump has made it increasingly clear he's not happy about this. Nonetheless, congressional oversight is written into the Constitution, and complying with it is part of the president's job. Every parent knows that the way to handle a 3-year-old throwing a tantrum isn't to give in. And make no mistake, Trump's blanket refusal to comply with congressional subpoenas and oversight efforts is not a reasoned defense of presidential prerogative. It's a tantrum. It's now the job of Congress to make sure that the president eats his peas.

Let's honor defenders of democracy
The flip side of vigorous oversight is rewarding those who step up to defend our democratic institutions despite the pressure they face. Congress — at least the House — should pass resolutions commending people like former White House counsel Don McGahn, former White House Deputy Chief of Staff Rick Dearborn and, yes, even former Attorney General Jeff Sessions. Other organizations who believe in our institutions should do the same.

This isn't about Republicans and Democrats or even liberals and conservatives. You can reject Sessions' politics while still cheering him for his steadfast defense of an independent and apolitical Justice Department. When we honor people who have served in the military, we don't ask about their politics before we thank them for their service — because their service to this country transcends politics. The same principle applies here.

There might come a time when Trump becomes even more of a danger than he is now and impeachment will need to be reconsidered. We aren't there yet. But that doesn't mean we can relax. It has been said that "the price of liberty is eternal vigilance." Here's another piece of that quote: "Only by continued oversight can the one in office be prevented from hardening into a despot."

That's good advice and certainly worth a try. The president won't like having Congress peering over his shoulder, but it's far better, both for Trump and for America, than the alternative.

Chris Truax, a member of USA TODAY's Board of Contributors, is a Republican and an appellate lawyer in San Diego.

Trump-whispering 101: Barr gives him 3rd Mueller investigation probe for his 2020 campaign

USA Today, May 17, 2019
By Chris Truax

Why launch overlapping investigations before the first is done? Maybe to ensure that client from hell can spin a campaign narrative for 18 months.

Every lawyer has had to deal with difficult clients. There's always someone who is demanding, wants unreasonable things, refuses to follow your advice and then blames you when things go wrong. Lawyers have to spend a lot of time and effort trying to keep these clients happy, or at least calm. By all accounts, Donald Trump has always been the client from hell, even before he was president.

Trump is not Attorney General William Barr's client. The United States of America is his client. Nonetheless, in his short career in the Trump administration, Barr has gone out of his way to mollify the president on multiple occasions. A case in point is his appointment of John Durham, a long-time Department of Justice attorney and currently the chief federal prosecutor for Connecticut, to investigate the origins of what eventually became the Mueller investigation, and related FBI surveillance activities. The first thing to keep in mind is that this is the third investigation into this "issue." The first is being overseen by the Office of the Inspector General for the Department of Justice. The

OIG regularly investigates how DOJ business is being conducted. While it investigates allegations of wrongdoing, it also makes recommendations about how to improve processes and policies within the DOJ. It's not at all uncommon for the OIG to do such an investigation in the aftermath of a particularly controversial or high-stakes probe. The office did one, for example, on the Clinton email investigation.

Jeff Sessions launched the second investigation back in March 2018, while he was attorney general, for the same reason Barr launched the third one just a few days ago: to try to keep Trump happy. Sessions appointed John Huber, the top federal prosecutor for Utah, to conduct more or less the same investigation Durham has just been handed.

Political theater based on conspiracy theories
These serial, overlapping investigations are troubling if for no other reason than they give the impression that they are meant to provide a narrative and make sure it continues until the 2020 election. It's hard to justify launching a third investigation before you've gotten the results of the first two — unless your goal is to keep the investigations running rather than to conclude them.

The second thing to remember is that these investigations are largely political theater. This is where I should explain to you exactly what the "issue" is that's being investigated.
I'm not going to do that because you can't explain half-baked conspiracy theories and it's dangerous to try.

Instead, I'm going to hand you a few useful tools that

will help you cut your way through the fog of hysteria being pushed by Trump and his surrogates.

Rule 1: Anytime someone feels the need to use the phrase "Hillary's email" in connection with the origins of the Mueller investigation, you can stop listening. This is pure *whataboutism* in its most ridiculous form.

Rule 2: Follow the rule of "Yes. And so?" Assume, for the sake of argument, that the allegations being made were true. Would it invalidate any of the conclusions of the Mueller investigation? Special counsel Mueller uncovered a massive Russian attack on the 2016 elections. It was, without question, a deadly serious conspiracy, even if the Trump campaign wasn't technically part of it. Mueller exposed this plot and filed over 30 criminal indictments regarding it. If he had not conducted his investigation, we wouldn't know about any of it and we would be utterly defenceless when the Russians try to do it all again in 2020. Certainly, Trump would never have organized such a thorough investigation into Russia's interference himself. He doesn't even want to admit that it happened.

It's the FBI's job to investigate
However the FBI was alerted to Russia's attack on our democracy, the agency was duty-bound to investigate when it caught wind of it. That's not "spying," as Barr called it, that's a counterintelligence investigation. Once the FBI had uncovered evidence that the Russians were actively attempting to infiltrate an American presidential campaign, would you really expect them to look the other way?

Rule 3: No harm, no foul. The general complaint underlying all these theories seems to be that the FBI was out to "get" Trump and prevent him from becoming president, by fair means or foul. And yet, the FBI kept an incredibly tight lid on its investigation, and none of the extremely damaging allegations it had uncovered became public until after the election — and this includes the now-famous "Steele dossier." It's nonsense to suggest there was some enormous plot to dig up dirt on Trump but then only release that information after the election was over.

The Department of Justice and the FBI are fiercely dedicated to defending America and providing scrupulous and apolitical justice. That's their job. As everyone working at those organizations is human, sometimes they make mistakes. And if they do, the DOJ's Office of the Inspector General will investigate and bring those mistakes to light. That's their job.

But there is no point in launching multiple investigations into the same issue, and certainly not until the OIG has completed the one it is doing. Starting an investigation just for the purpose of suggesting that there's something to investigate — which is what Barr has done — is a dangerous step toward turning the Department of Justice into a political tool. When it comes to Barr's investigation into the origins of the Mueller investigation, where there's smoke, there's mirrors. Don't fall for it.

Chris Truax, a member of USA TODAY's Board of Contributors and an appellate lawyer in San Diego, is on the legal advisory board of Republicans for the Rule of Law.

Fear, not outrage: Trump doesn't get better, he just makes the people around him worse

USA Today, June 17, 2019
By Chris Truax

The Russia collusion suspicions were fueled entirely by Trump and his campaign. The ABC News foreign 'dirt' interview shows he hasn't learned a thing.

A lot of people are outraged by President Donald Trump's admission last week that he would happily accept dirt on a political opponent from a foreign government.

I'm not outraged though, or even particularly upset. This is nothing new. Trump has said as much over and over again. Almost a year ago, he tweeted about the infamous Trump Tower meeting with Russians promising dirt on Hillary Clinton, "This was a meeting to get information on an opponent, totally legal and done all the time in politics."

What I am is frightened. After two years of being hectored, lectured and dragged over the coals, Trump has learned absolutely nothing. Worse, he doesn't appear to have the capacity or desire to learn anything. Most people learn pretty quickly about touching a hot stove.

In Trump's case, his campaign's efforts to get a foreign government to give him dirt on a political opponent

have been more like licking a frozen flagpole —
incredibly stupid and hard to escape.

Trump himself fuels collusion suspicions

Trump's constant complaints about being suspected of
colluding with the Russians were entirely fueled by
Trump and his own campaign. Who can forget the news
conference where he encouraged the Russians to hack
into Clinton's servers and steal her emails? Donald
Trump Jr.'s giddy acceptance of an apparent offer from
the Russian government promising dirt on Clinton and
her campaign? George Papadopoulos bragging to an
Australian diplomat that Russia had Clinton's emails,
which is how the inquiry that became the Mueller
investigation got started in the first place?

Wanted, a patriotic president: Trump invites foreigners to distort 2020 elections. Why won't he protect his own country?

Apparently, it's Trump himself who forgets all these
things and the fallout that came with them. The Mueller
report isn't a vindication of Trump's conduct. Under
the most imaginative pro-Trump reading possible, it's
still a dire warning. Trump and his campaign avoided a
felony conspiracy with the Russian government by pure
dumb luck.

When a furor erupted over his comments to ABC News
last week, Trump tried and failed to walk them back:
"Of course" he'd look at the information, but "of
course" he'd report it to law enforcement — "if I
thought anything was incorrect or badly stated." But it
has been explained to him time and time again: Whether
or not you report it to the FBI, which even Steve

Bannon agrees is the only decent, American thing to do, accepting compromising information about a political opponent from a foreign government is a crime that can earn you up to five years in a federal prison. This is not a controversial position. The FBI says so. Even Sen. Lindsey Graham of South Carolina, a staunch Trump ally, says so.

'I would not have thought I needed to say this'
In the words of Ellen Weintraub, the head of the Federal Election Commission (appointed by Republican George W. Bush, if it matters), "Let me make something 100% clear to the American public and anyone running for public office: It is illegal for any person to solicit, accept, or receive anything of value from a foreign national in connection with a U.S. election." She introduced the statement on Twitter with: "I would not have thought that I needed to say this."

If the Trump campaign had succeeded in its desperate quest to get the Russian government to turn over dirt on Clinton, a lot more people from the Trump campaign would be in prison today, including Donald Trump Jr. Most people would be sobered by such a near-death experience. Not Trump.

Honor among partisans: Trump calls foreign intelligence 'oppo research.' I call it illegal, and I should know.
"It's not interference. They have information. I think I'd take it. If I thought there was something wrong, I'd go maybe to the FBI, if I thought there was something wrong. But when somebody comes up with oppo research, right, they come up with oppo research."

I can almost hear people shrugging. "Oh, that's just Trump being Trump! You have to take him seriously, not literally." Sorry, but no. When the president says something like this, it has consequences. Here's what Kayleigh McEnany, speaking for Trump's reelection campaign, had to say on Thursday evening about following the president's "directives" about campaign assistance from a foreign government.

Trump campaign's legal director is, alas, Trump
"We follow his lead. The president is our leader, we follow everything he says, his directives," McEnany told CBSN. "President Trump is the communications director. He's the political director. He's the leader of our campaign. So we follow and echo what he says."

Most unfortunately, Trump also seems to be the campaign's legal director. In plain language, Trump instructed his campaign to commit a felony, and the spokesperson for the campaign responded, "Yes, my leader!" I cannot think of a single more chilling thing I have ever seen in modern American political discourse. In the words of Don McGahn, the president's ex-White House counsel, Trump is asking his people to do "crazy sh--." But unlike McGahn, they no longer have the moral intelligence to say no.

Usually, I like to end this sort of things with a suggestion about what can be done to fix the problem. But this time, I've got nothing. We have a president who can't or won't learn from his mistakes and a large group of people fanatically devoted to that president who can no longer tell right from wrong. Trump isn't going to get better. He only makes the people around him worse. I genuinely do not know what the solution is. But I do know that we had better find one.

Chris Truax, a member of USA TODAY's Board of Contributors and an appellate lawyer in San Diego, is on the legal advisory board of Republicans for the Rule of Law.

Busing was divisive even among liberals. Biden, Harris and all of us should move on.

USA Today, July 2, 2019
By Chris Truax

Detroit Mayor Coleman Young and other black leaders opposed forced busing. It was decades ago and complicated. Democrats need to focus on the future.

For a while now, the most demanding wing of the progressive movement has been gunning for Thomas Jefferson. Their feeling is that because he was a slave owner, his contributions to the American experiment should no longer be recognized and celebrated. This is, of course, ridiculous.

Anyone trying to quote "all men are created equal" back at Thomas Jefferson is either a fool or a hypocrite. Jefferson lived in different times and different conditions, and it is absurd to judge him by our standards of enlightenment. To paraphrase Isaac Newton, if we have seen further than others, it is because we have stood on the shoulders of giants. And in American history, they don't come much taller than Thomas Jefferson.

I'm not particularly bothered by this. Despite the judgment of groups like the Democratic Party of New Hampshire, I'm confident that Jefferson's contributions will stand the test of time. But now this same sort of ahistorical Monday-morning quarterbacking is starting to affect real people in real time.

Biden attacked for view on forced busing
Former Vice President Joe Biden is under attack because in the 1970s, he had the "wrong" position on forced busing. It seems progressives are now in favor of busing. Biden was against it. In their view, this renders Biden out of step with the Democratic Party and is unacceptable in a presidential nominee.

As with their rejection of Jefferson, this completely ignores historical context. In the 1970s, busing was an incredibly contentious and complicated issue with even the most committed liberals — that's what progressives called themselves then — lined up on both sides. Detroit is a case in point.

Coleman Young had impeccable liberal credentials. In 1952, he came to national attention for publicly spitting in the eye of the House Un-American Activities Committee. In 1963, he was elected to the Michigan Senate. In 1969, he became the Senate minority leader, where he helped pass a law that blocked the forcible reassignment of thousands of Detroit students.

Young had one more noteworthy achievement: He became Detroit's first African-American mayor.

Forced busing divided black people
Forced busing was a divisive issue, even within the black community. In 1971, that bill blocking the reassignment of all those Detroit students passed with the support of all but one member of the Michigan legislature's Black Caucus. African Americans opposed

busing for a variety of reasons. Some were in favor of local control. Some thought the correct solution was providing more resources for primarily black schools. Others were concerned that forced busing often resulted in local schools simply closing down and the students distributed to schools far outside the community.

As the mayor of Detroit, Young continued to oppose forced busing. He even filed a brief opposing a case brought by the NAACP that sought to use busing to integrate the Detroit school system.

Was Mayor Young right? I don't know. But none of the modern progressives criticizing his position know, either. He dealt with these decisions in real time, addressing the concerns of real people. It was a complicated, messy problem with no perfect solution. It's incredibly patronizing to claim that people like Coleman Young "didn't get it," even with the arrogance of hindsight. When that hindsight ignores a complex and often inconvenient history, it isn't just patronizing; it's shameful.

Coleman Young and Joe Biden were both deeply committed to civil rights, integration and equality. They had, however, a different view on the best way to achieve that than do the latest crop of progressive activists. A little humility is called for. For us, forced busing was something we read about in history books. Donald Trump doesn't even know what it is. But for Young and Biden, it was a lived experience. We can't say we would have unquestionably come to a different decision had we been in their shoes.

There is a grubby and unpleasant political feel to these attacks. On Friday, the Rev. Jesse Jackson criticized Biden's long-ago opinions on busing, claiming that he was on "the wrong side of history." Many progressives know nothing about forced busing except what they've read on the internet. But Jackson is old enough to know just how divided the black community was.

Challenge Biden over future, not past
Jackson attended and addressed the 1972 National Black Political Convention in Gary, Indiana, which drew some 10,000 delegates and observers from across the country, according to the Indiana Historical Bureau. The group passed a resolution opposing busing that some of them disapproved so strongly, they walked out, The New York Times wrote.

Jackson himself supported black self-determination and black control over black education back then and gave a rousing speech to that effect, the historical bureau reported, based on accounts from the time. Today he could be the voice of wisdom and experience to explain that busing was difficult and controversial. Sadly, he has chosen not to do it, and our political discourse is poorer for this.

If Biden's armor is a little scratched and dented, it's because he has been through the wars. I disagree with many of Biden's political positions. But I recognize that he came to those positions thoughtfully and in good faith. I also recognize that throughout his career, Biden has been willing to grapple with difficult questions wiser politicians would have avoided. This makes him politically vulnerable. It also makes him a leader.

Democrats have one job in 2020, beating Donald Trump. They aren't going to accomplish that by having an ideological beauty contest, and they aren't going to accomplish that by ignoring facts and twisting history to fit a convenient political narrative. If Sen. Kamala Harris or anyone else wants to take down Joe Biden, they need to do it on their visions for the future, not by refighting the battles of decades ago.

Chris Truax, a Republican, is a member of USA TODAY's Board of Contributors and an appellate lawyer in San Diego.

Republican: I'm telling Democrats how to beat Trump in 2020. It's Job One so get over it.

USA Today, July 12, 2019
By Chris Truax

Enough with the progressive wish lists, just focus on winning. The next president is everyone's business, and we can't afford to screw it up. Again.

There is an old saying that it is permissible to walk with the devil when crossing a narrow bridge. Welcome, progressives, to the 2020 presidential election.

First, let's get one thing out of the way. Yes, I'm a Republican. And yes, as someone staunchly opposed to what Donald Trump is doing to America's institutions, I'm going to give Democrats advice on who they should be nominating for president.

Like it or not, the Democratic party has had greatness thrust upon it. Every American who believes in the basic foundations of the American experiment, things like the rule of law, the Constitution and an apolitical Justice Department, now has a stake in who Democrats nominate in 2020. So please stop telling fellow travelers like me to mind our own business and start taking on board some of what we are saying. The next president of the United States is everyone's business, and we can't afford to screw it up. Again.

Trump is enough to fire up Democrats

America needs you to focus. Democrats' first thought in the morning and their last thought when they fall asleep at night should be, "How will this play in Erie, Pennsylvania?"

There are four states that matter in 2020: Wisconsin, Michigan, Pennsylvania and Florida. Win three out of four of those states and Trump is a one-term president. No matter how popular something might be with activists in Los Angeles or donors in Manhattan, it's dead weight or worse if it isn't a winner with Rotary Club members in Kenosha, Wisconsin.

So don't treat this like a base election. Democrats are already guaranteed a nominee that will excite their base and drive a big turnout. His name is Donald Trump. Getting activists "excited" by bold policy positions is a waste of time. You could get every Democrat in California so excited that they all voted twice and it would make not the slightest difference to the outcome of the election. All that matters is getting voters in Michigan who have become uncomfortable and disenchanted with Donald Trump to vote for you once.

The people you really have to motivate aren't the Democratic base, they're the people in the middle who have been unsettled by Trump's presidency. They can see what Trump is and will happily vote for a reasonable alternative. But if Democrats offer what appears to them as a choice between death by hanging and death by firing squad, a lot of them will just give up and not vote at all.

Far-left ideas will boost Trump
Democrats could, however, easily expand this four-state map — for the Republicans. Want to put Minnesota, Colorado, Nevada and New Hampshire in play? Easy. Just run on policies like eliminating private health insurance, reparations for slavery, legalizing drugs and decriminalizing prostitution. Every one of these projects has been pushed by one or more Democratic presidential candidates. There may be things to be said for all of these issues. And someday, we should have a serious policy debate about them. Today is not that day.

Those legendary soccer moms are still out there and, by and large, they have had enough of Trump's antics. But if you want to run on far-left positions like, say, resurrecting forced busing, they're going to stick with the devil they know rather than vote for someone who promises to do things like send their kids on 30-mile bus rides every day.

This doesn't mean Democrats can't run on progressive policies. Talk about fixing and expanding Obamacare, if you want. Talk about universal pre-kindergarten. Talk about guaranteed parental leave. If it's OK with those voters in Erie, it's OK with me.

Progressives keep trying to convince themselves that people are sick and tired of what's going on in this country. They are half right. Americans are tired. They're tired of the endless rancor, the name-calling and the lies. They're tired of the frenetic insanity of the last few years and the unprecedented attacks on America's institutions. Americans don't want to burn down the system. They want to put the fire out. Progressive activists may be angry but most of us are just exhausted.

Don't mess this up for America
Democrats have one job in 2020: Beating Donald Trump. Nothing else matters. If progressives manage to mess this up by insisting on hard-left positions and ideological purity, they will own Trump's second term. There is a time and a place for everything. When the ship is sinking and you find yourself in a lifeboat, you don't argue about where you want to go, you head for the nearest land. Further travel arrangements can wait until you're back in civilization.

The 2020 election is not a normal election. It isn't going to be about progressives and conservatives. It's going to be about those who believe America's democratic institutions are more important than the politics of the day and those who are willing to wreck them for short-term political gain. We who choose to stand with our democratic institutions need to keep our eye on the prize. We can't afford the self-indulgence of standing on principle and going down in glorious defeat.

Or rather, we must all stand on one overriding principle, that we must install someone with respect for the rule of law and reverence for our constitutional system of government as the next president of the United States. That will require compromise from all of us. The bridge is long and narrow, but cross it we must.

Republican Chris Truax, an appellate lawyer in San Diego, is a member of USA TODAY's Board of Contributors.

There are a few (Dozen?) Glitches in that Donald Trump plan to end birthright citizenship

USA Today, August 27, 2019
By Chris Truax

From the Constitution and the Supreme Court to diplomatic immunity and Italian ancestry, it's complicated. And it's another way to torment Obama.

When it comes to news, August is traditionally the silly season and President Donald Trump certainly did his part last week to lighten the national mood. He got into a fight with the Danish prime minister because she wouldn't sell him Greenland, said he wanted to award himself the Medal of Honor, and endorsed the claim that "Jewish people in Israel ... love him like he is the second coming of God."

It's possible that the Greenland idea was serious. He did cancel a state visit because of it. But all the rest was clearly parody. How stupid would you have to be to think Israeli Jews would be excited about "the second coming of God?" I mean, if you're Jewish, that's not even a thing.

If you are a lawyer, the most hilarious thing Trump did last week was his shtick about eliminating birthright citizenship by executive order. Now, it is true that lawyers can have an odd sense of humor, but this is a joke that, with a little explanation, can be enjoyed by lawyers and nonlawyers alike.

'Birthies' want to redefine citizenship

While the people opposed to it do their best to make it appear as if there's an actual debate, the basics of birthright citizenship are pretty straightforward. The 14th Amendment says, "All persons born or naturalized in the United States, and subject to the jurisdiction thereof, are citizens of the United States and of the state wherein they reside."

Trump and many of his fans don't like the U.S. version of birthright citizenship because it means that every child born on U.S. soil is automatically granted U.S. citizenship, even if their parents are here illegally or as tourists. They think this is crazy and want to end it.

Let's call them "birthies." They have decided that "subject to the jurisdiction thereof" means that only those "not owing allegiance to anybody else" and "not subject to some foreign power" are automatically granted birthright citizenship.

Apparently, if I follow the logic, the idea is that if your parents are here illegally, they are citizens of someplace else. Therefore, when you're born, you are a citizen of someplace else and, therefore, owe allegiance to somebody else and, so, you don't qualify as a citizen under the 14th Amendment.

Now, the fun begins. As it turns out, just like the children of illegal immigrants, tens of millions of people born in the United States to U.S. citizens are also citizens of another country at birth even if they don't know it. Lots of countries automatically confer citizenship based on who your parents were. Some countries make you automatic citizens if one of your grandparents was a citizen. In the case of Italy, you may be an Italian citizen if any of your ancestors was an Italian citizen going right back to the founding of Italy.

Settled for all time in 1898: Trump challenges Constitution with talk of an executive order to end birthright citizenship

Under the birthies' reading of the 14th Amendment, none of these people would be U.S. citizens because, at birth, they would be citizens of another country. We always thought there was something sketchy about Nancy Pelosi!

Another way to torment Obama

You know who else wouldn't be a U.S. citizen? Former President Barack Obama. His father was a Kenyan national, and Kenya automatically confers citizenship on all children born to Kenyan parents. I'm sure the birthies would consider this a feature, not a bug. Poor Obama. First they claim he wasn't a citizen because he wasn't born in America. Now they're claiming he shouldn't be a citizen even though he was. These people never quit!

Luckily for Obama and House Speaker Pelosi, this reading of the 14th Amendment is nonsense. In the 1898 decision United States v. Wong Kim Ark, the Supreme Court explained what "subject to the jurisdiction of the United States" means. A person is subject to the jurisdiction of the United States when they are subject to the laws of the United States. Nothing more. Nothing less.

Changing Constitution by executive order: This election is a referendum on Trump's corrosive impact on our politics

Birthies claim this case doesn't actually endorse birthright citizenship for the children of illegal immigrants because Ark's parents were legal permanent residents. But that's irrelevant, both under the 14th Amendment and the reasoning in the Ark decision. You can squint at the language of the amendment as hard as you like, and you won't see one word about your parents. The only thing that matters is whether you are subject to the jurisdiction of the United States. Your parents have nothing to do with it ... with one exception.

We'll always have Greenland

Part of what makes this so funny, at least if you are a lawyer, is that Congress could eliminate birthright citizenship if it wanted to. No constitutional amendment is required. In fact, it has already done so in some cases. Children born to accredited diplomats are entitled to the same diplomatic immunity granted to their parents. As the Ark case makes clear, to end birthright citizenship, all you have to do is confer diplomatic immunity on every child born to an illegal immigrant. Problem solved!

Of course, placing children outside the laws of the United States based on the nationality of their parents has its own constitutional problems. As Mark Twain said, however, it's best not to examine a good joke too closely.

Sadly, summer will soon be a memory and we'll all have

to turn our attention to serious matters like raising tariffs on Chinese Christmas decorations in support of the U.S. twinkle-light industry. But we all needed a break, and this comic interlude was nice while it lasted. No doubt, things will get pretty serious in the months ahead. At least we'll always have Greenland.

Chris Truax, an appellate lawyer in San Diego, is an adviser to Republicans for the Rule of Law and a member of USA TODAY's Board of Contributors.

Sharpiegate: Trump pressure to bend weather facts is abuse of power. Expect more in 2020.

USA Today, September 12, 2019
By Chris Truax

Trump's desire to politicize everything will get worse as 2020 heats up. The hurricane debacle is a chance for Congress to expose this misconduct.

President Donald Trump crossed into literal old-man-yells-at-clouds territory with his one-man crusade to retroactively change the weather. For a while, it was all very amusing, in a baffling sort of way. But nobody's laughing now.

Inaccurate weather information can endanger lives. And new reports this week suggest that Trump was not only wrong, he and members of his administration also pressured scientists to back him and undercut the front-line weather forecasters at the National Weather Service.

"Sharpiegate" began with Trump's Sept. 1 tweet that Alabama was in the path of Hurricane Dorian. "In addition to Florida - South Carolina, North Carolina, Georgia, and Alabama, will most likely be hit (much) harder than anticipated. Looking like one of the largest hurricanes ever. Already category 5. BE CAREFUL! GOD BLESS EVERYONE!"

Within 20 minutes, the National Weather Service in

Birmingham, desperate not to cause unnecessary panic, sent out a tweet correcting the president's error: "Alabama will NOT see any impacts from #Dorian. We repeat, no impacts from Hurricane #Dorian will be felt across Alabama. The system will remain too far east."

Mistakes like this can happen, especially when you are trying to get a handle on events in real time. The important thing is that those mistakes are corrected, as happened here. Anyone else would have shrugged their shoulders and moved on. Not Trump.

A few days later, in a bizarre effort to convince America that Alabama really had been at risk from Hurricane Dorian, Trump appeared in the Oval Office with an official National Oceanic and Atmospheric Administration map that had been altered with a felt tip pen.

Even that wasn't enough. Trump spent the week insisting again and again that he was right. All this culminated last Friday with an unsigned statement from NOAA that said Trump had been right on Sept. 1 and the National Weather Service was wrong.

Just the start of bending truth

The statement pointed to models showing that, when Trump sent his tweet, there was a less than 10% probability of a tiny sliver of Eastern Alabama seeing winds of at least 39 miles per hour. So National Weather Service forecasters were absolutely correct to publicly contradict Trump's freelance hurricane warning. It was shameful for NOAA to throw them under the bus because somebody was afraid of Trump. NOAA knows this perfectly well. There's a reason the statement wasn't signed.

You would have hoped that if there were one area of government activity immune to improper presidential influence, it would be predicting the weather, but no. In fact, new reports Wednesday in The Washington Post and The New York Times, citing unnamed senior administration officials and people familiar with the events, suggest that Trump himself, directly and indirectly, pressured his staff and appointees to contradict the Birmingham forecasters.

All of this is cause for grave concern.
First, it's a public display of Trump's flagrant disregard for expertise and his refusal to admit error under any circumstances. It was amusing to see him show an old weather map hand-corrected with a Sharpie. Will he do the same thing with intelligence data regarding North Korea's missile program? That wouldn't be quite so hilarious.

Second, Trump's apparent willingness to force federal agencies like NOAA to publicly bend the truth in support of his favorite version of reality is unlikely to be limited to weather maps. Does anyone really think that he won't apply the same pressures to the Bureau of Labor Statistics if the unemployment figures start to "contradict" him, or the Bureau of Economic Analysis if growth starts to slow?

Finally, it has become increasingly obvious over the past few weeks that there's something very, very wrong with the president, and it's getting worse. His obsession — there's no other word for it — with convincing people that he was correct about Alabama being in Dorian's path is deeply unsettling.

Expose improper influence

Perhaps most disturbing of all is Trump's belief that his hand-corrected weather map would somehow be proof of something. This is delusional and pretty strong evidence of an inability to engage in critical thinking. His claim that he had never heard of an actual Category 5 hurricane even though there have been three other Category 5 hurricanes during his presidency is further evidence of serious cognitive dysfunction. Hurricane Michael was still a Category 5 hurricane when it made landfall in Florida. This isn't the sort of thing a person forgets, especially a person in charge of disaster response.

In an email to his staff that was later made public, Craig McLean, NOAA's assistant administrator for research, said he is investigating the "very concerning" episode. Beyond that, Sharpiegate gives Congress a perfect opportunity to pry the lid off the problem of improper presidential influence. There's no classified data involved here, and even Trump can't claim executive privilege over weather reports or efforts to get them changed after the fact.

Trump's willingness to politicize everything from the Justice Department to the National Weather Service is going to be an increasingly serious problem as we head into the 2020 election. Exposing the details of his efforts to influence NOAA to some congressional sunshine will send a message: There will be accountability, so mind what you do. Congress may not be able to stop Trump from lying. But maybe it can help ordinary federal employees stand up for the truth.

Chris Truax, an appellate lawyer in San Diego, is an adviser to Republicans for the Rule of Law and a member of USA TODAY's Board of Contributors.

If you liked these opinion pieces, write a review on Amazon, so that all the Munchkins in the Land of US can be encouraged to read them too!

www.ingramcontent.com/pod-product-compliance
Lightning Source LLC
Chambersburg PA
CBHW030252030426
42336CB00009B/362